ROCK TRIVIA
MADNESS

60S TO 90S ROCK MUSIC
TRIVIA & AMAZING FACTS

MUSIC TRIVIA VOL 1

BY
BILL O'NEILL & RAY CONNOR

DON'T FORGET YOUR FREE BOOKS

CONTENTS

INTRODUCTION

Back in early March 1951, Ike Turner and his backing band, the Kings of Rhythm, were recording at the now-legendary Sun Studios in Memphis, Tennessee. The song wasn't anything too special—a jump blues number about the Oldsmobile 88 car (also known as the "Rocket 88").

There was a slight problem, though. The cone in guitarist Willie Kizart's amplifier had somehow come loose (it might have happened while the band was driving down Highway 61). The people in the studio tried stuffing wadded-up pieces of newspaper into the amp to hold the cone in place. This made the amp give off a distorted noise. Producer Sam Phillips liked the sound and decided to include it in the record.

The final single, "Rocket 88," became a number one hit and one of the very first records to feature distorted guitar. Many critics have cited it as the first rock and roll record ever made.

Regardless of whether or not it's the first, "Rocket 88" pointed the way towards the future. Starting in the mid-50s, a new kind of music would emerge that took from blues, country, R&B, and other genres and infused those elements with a startling freshness and power. In the decades that followed, rock and roll would spread across the world and give birth to a bewildering variety of subgenres. It has influenced practically every aspect of Western society and culture as we know it today.

Let's take a look at some of the artists who have kept rock and roll alive and exciting over the years. You'll learn amazing facts like:

- How a backup musician for a largely forgotten R&B group became the most idolized and influential rock guitarist of all time.
- How a glam rock icon almost gave up fame and fortune to become a monk.
- How a joke about deodorant inspired the name of a single that changed rock.

Are you ready to rock? Here we go!

CHAPTER ONE

ARTISTS OF THE 60S

"Rock and roll is here to stay," Danny and the Juniors sang in 1958. The 1960s proved them right.

The music pioneered in the 1950s by artists like Elvis Presley, Chuck Berry, and Little Richard became a worldwide phenomenon in the decade that followed. It produced numerous subgenres, influenced all aspects of popular culture, and signaled a change in thinking and values between the older and younger generations. Here are some interesting facts on a few of the artists that made the 60s so exciting.

BOB DYLAN

No 60s songwriter is more revered than Bob Dylan. His songs have influenced countless artists (including many of the people we'll look at later) and received mountains of awards, including the Nobel Prize for Literature in 2016. Yet despite all the accolades and adoration, Dylan has always forged his own path (who else would shrug off calls from the Nobel Prize committee?).

Though he first became famous as a folksinger, Dylan loved rock and roll from a young age. Growing up in Minnesota, he formed numerous rock bands as a teenager. These early musical endeavors didn't impress everybody. During a high school talent show performance, he reportedly had his microphone cut for playing too loud.

In retrospect, that might have been a sign of things to come. After penning such now-classic folk anthems as "Blowin' in the Wind," "A Hard Rain's a Gonna Fall," and "The Times They are a-Changin'," Dylan switched back to rock in the mid-60s. This aroused the ire of many in the folk music scene. During his electric set at the 1965 Newport Folk Festival, folksinger Pete Seeger said he wanted to cut Dylan's mic cable with an axe. People have given various reasons why Seeger said this and why people in the audience booed during the set. But here's the main takeaway: Dylan's never been afraid to stir things up.

THE BEATLES

From singing and songwriting to instrumentation and album production, the Beatles changed everything. Even after more than half a century, they remain the bestselling rock group of all time. In their early days, however, no one could've guessed the heights they'd reach.

The band that eventually became the Beatles started out playing skiffle music, an amalgam of jazz, blues, and folk. Back then, the lads from Liverpool really were just lads too—John Lennon was only 16 when he started the group, and Paul McCartney and George Harrison were 15 and 14 when they joined.

As for the name "Beatles," Lennon and original bassist Stuart Sutcliffe came up with it as a nod to Buddy Holly and the Crickets. Before that, they'd gone by the Quarrymen and Johnny and the Moondogs. It's safe to say they picked the name with staying power.

THE ROLLING STONES

You might argue whether the Rolling Stones are, as they bill themselves, "The World's Greatest Rock and Roll Band." However, few would disagree that they're one of the best. Aside from their sort-of rivals the Beatles, no other British Invasion group wrote as many classic songs or had as far-reaching influence.

While original manager Andrew Loog Oldham conceived of them as scruffy bad boys in contrast to the clean-cut Beatles, the Fab Four did the Stones a big solid early in their career. John Lennon and Paul McCartney gave Jagger, Richards, and company the song "I Wanna Be Your Man" to record in 1963. It hit number 12 on the UK music charts.

"The thing is, with the Beatles and us, it was always a very friendly relationship," Keith Richards remembered in his autobiography *Life* (2010). "It was also very cannily worked out, because in those days singles were coming out every six, eight weeks. And we'd try and time it so that we didn't clash."

Pretty courteous for a bunch of bad boys. By the way, it was The Beatles who first recommended that Oldham check out the Stones.

THE WHO

Back in the 60s and early 70s, the Who was one of the most dynamic rock bands in the world. They developed a reputation for destroying their equipment onstage and their hotel rooms offstage. They created plenty of stuff too, of course, including iconic songs like "My Generation," "Anyway, Anyhow, Anywhere," and "I Can See for Miles." These singles and albums like *The Who Sell Out* (1967) and *Tommy* (1969) inspired numerous punk and hard rock groups to start kicking out the jams.

While lead guitarist and songwriter Pete Townshend would become known as the main creative force behind the Who, lead singer Roger Daltrey actually served as the band's leader in the early days. It was Daltrey who originally formed the group in the late 1950s. They went by the name "The Detours" at first, but they needed to change it after discovering a group with a similar moniker. Townshend wanted to call the band "The Hair," but his roommate Richard Barnes suggested "The Who." Time has shown which was the better choice.

THE BEACH BOYS

Formed in 1961, the Beach Boys were the most popular surf group in the world thanks to hits like "Surfin' Safari," "California Girls," and "Surfin' USA." At the height of their popularity, they were the only American group to rival the Beatles. Paul McCartney himself has called the Beach Boys' *Pet Sounds*

(1966) as one of his favorite albums of all time (as well as the inspiration for *Sgt. Pepper*).

Today, the Beach Boys' main songwriter, Brian Wilson, is widely revered for his production and arrangement genius. Wilson had to work hard to achieve his ideal of pop perfection, though. One of the group's biggest hits, "Good Vibrations," took seven months to complete. He recorded tracks at several different studios and, by his own estimate, spent $50,000-$75,000 (according to *The Wall Street Journal*, that figure would translate to more than $400,000 today). That's a lot of time and money to devote to four minutes and fifteen seconds!

JIMI HENDRIX

The 60s produced a lot of guitar gods, but Jimi Hendrix tops them all. Over the course of four years and four official albums (not to mention a plethora of posthumous releases), Hendrix expanded the possibilities of the electric guitar. He marshaled feedback and other sound effects to create rock and roll of nearly unprecedented power. The Rock and Roll Hall of Fame called him "the most gifted instrumentalist of all time."

Hendrix is so singular a figure that it's hard to picture him serving as a sideman for anyone, but that's exactly what he did in the early 60s, playing in the backing bands for Wilson Pickett, Sam Cooke, the Isley Brothers, and others. It wasn't until Keith Richards' then-girlfriend Linda Keith saw him perform with Curtis Knight and the Squires in 1966 that people truly began to recognize his phenomenal talent.

JAMES BROWN

No overview of 60s popular music would be complete without a shout-out to the Godfather of Soul. Beginning with his smash 1965 hit "Papa's Got a Brand New Bag," James Brown would transform traditional R&B into what would become known as funk. The Rolling Stones and the Who were already hip to his music, but Brown's groundbreaking 60s and 70s recordings would inspire other rock bands and pave the way for disco, hip-hop, and a lot of what dominates the charts today.

However, none of Brown's achievements may have occurred if it weren't for one teenage connection. Brown was doing time at the Boys Industrial Training Institute in Georgia in 1951 when he befriended a young gospel and pop singer named Bobby Byrd—he's the guy singing with Brown on the funk classic "Get Up (I Feel Like Being a) Sex Machine". Byrd's family and church helped sponsor Brown's release from the institute. Once he got out, Brown and Byrd started performing together, and the rest is history.

THE GRATEFUL DEAD

No band of the 60s or any other era epitomizes the concept of "jam band" better than the Grateful Dead. Formed in 1965, the San Francisco band became legendary for their concerts' long instrumental jams.

Though inspired in part by the Beatles and various early rock and R&B artists, the Dead brought a wide range of influences into their music. Bassist Phil Lesh was a classically trained trumpeter. Rhythm guitarist Bob Weir brought jazz influences to his parts. Lead guitarist Jerry Garcia mashed together bluegrass, country, jazz, and rock. Promoter Bill Graham might have said it best: "They're not the best at what they do, they're the only ones at what they do."

THE BYRDS

Get out your dictionary and look up "folk rock." If you don't see a picture of the Byrds there, buy a new dictionary.

Just kidding. But seriously, the Los Angeles-based group pioneered the genre with hit covers of Bob Dylan's "Mr. Tambourine Man" and Pete Seeger's "Turn! Turn! Turn!" Songs like "Eight Miles High" and albums like *Sweetheart of the Rodeo* (1968) also established the band as one of the originators of psychedelic rock and country rock as well.

Rock and roll didn't come naturally to the Byrds. Founding members Roger McGuinn, Gene Clark, and David Crosby all came out of the coffeehouse and college folk scenes. Drummer Michael Clarke didn't even have a proper drum kit at first, just a tambourine and some cardboard boxes. In fact, only Roger McGuinn actually played on their single of "Mr. Tambourine Man." The other parts on the record were performed by a now-legendary team of session musicians called the Wrecking Crew, which included Leon Russell on piano.

BUFFALO SPRINGFIELD

Although they only lasted from 1966 to 1968, Buffalo Springfield is a crucial band in American rock history.

The group scored a hit with their protest song "For What It's Worth" but had very little commercial success besides that. Instead, many of Buffalo Springfield's members made it big after they broke up. Guitarist Stephen Stills joined ex-Byrd David Crosby and Graham Nash from British pop-rock group the Hollies to form the supergroup Crosby, Stills & Nash. Guitarist Richie Furay and bassist Jim Messina formed the country rock band Poco. Last but not least, guitarist Neil Young achieved superstar status both as part of Crosby, Stills, Nash & Young and as a solo artist.

In spite of these major talents, the true heart of Buffalo Springfield was original bassist Bruce Palmer. Palmer met Young in 1966. They played bass and guitar, respectively, in the Mynah Birds with future "Super Freak" funk star Rick James. After that group broke up, the two musicians moved to Los Angeles and met the other members of Buffalo Springfield. "Bruce would lay down a groove, and we could have done anything," Stills told *The Guardian*. "He was the focus that balanced Neil and me."

Unfortunately, drug arrests and other legal problems led to Palmer leaving the band in 1968. He died in 2004 of a heart attack. He never got close to the level of success that his former bandmates reached.

CREEDENCE CLEARWATER REVIVAL

In 1993, Bruce Springsteen inducted Creedence Clearwater Revival into the Rock and Roll Hall of Fame. "In the late 60s and early 70s," he said, "they weren't the hippest band in the world—just the best."

Some might argue that point, but there's no disputing that CCR came up with more than their share of classic tracks. "Bad Moon Rising," "Proud Mary," "Fortunate Son," "Who'll Stop the Rain"—the list goes on and on. In 1969 alone, they scored three Top Ten albums and four hit singles. John Fogerty's terse, smart songwriting and the band's mix of blues, country, R&B, and rockabilly still provide a touchstone for roots-rock and alt-country artists today.

CCR's no-frills, to-the-point songs contrasted sharply with the psychedelic excesses of other San Francisco rock groups. So, it may surprise some to learn that Fogerty and company actually played Woodstock in 1969! CCR took the stage very early on Sunday morning after a long set by the Grateful Dead. John Fogerty thought the performance sucked, so he refused to let the band appear in the Woodstock documentary or on its soundtrack.

THE YARDBIRDS

Today, the Yardbirds are probably best known for kick-starting the careers of three ace guitarists: Eric Clapton, Jeff Beck, and Jimmy Page. After the band broke up in 1968, Page recruited vocalist Robert Plant, bassist John Paul Jones, and drummer John

Bonham. The quartet started performing as the New Yardbirds but soon changed their name to Led Zeppelin.

Still, the Yardbirds achieved a fair amount of success in their day. They scored a handful of hits, including a cover of Bo Diddley's "I'm a Man" and "For Your Love." The latter song was written by Graham Gouldman, who would go on to form the art-pop group 10cc.

THE KINKS

While not quite on the same level as the Beatles or the Rolling Stones in terms of mainstream popularity, the Kinks' influence and body of work are certainly nothing to sniff at. Formed in 1964 by brothers Ray and Dave Davies, this British Invasion group had big hits both in the UK and the US like "You Really Got Me" and "Lola." The band's penchant for instantly identifiable riffs and lyrical depictions of English society and culture inspired both punk titans like the Clash and Britpop champions like Oasis and Blur.

Plenty of the Kinks' contemporaries took note of their work too. The Who's Pete Townshend consciously wrote "I Can't Explain" as an imitation of their style. Not only that, their raga-esque song "See My Friends" may have inspired the Beatles to dabble with Eastern music on *Sgt. Pepper* and *Rubber Soul* (1965).

"I remember it vividly, and still think it's a remarkable pop song," the Kinks' friend, artist Barry Fantoni, said. "I was with the Beatles the evening that they actually sat around listening to it on a gramophone, saying, 'You know, this guitar thing sounds like a sitar. We must get one of those.'"

THE DOORS

With their balance of experimentalism and pop savvy—as well as frontman Jim Morrison's moody, provocative lyrics and persona—the Doors was one of the hottest American rock bands of the 60s. From their founding in 1965 to Morrison's death in 1971, the group became known both for their alluring yet menacing music and for their rebellious, antagonistic stage antics.

During their tenure with Morrison, the Doors never had a steady bass player. In concert, organ player Ray Manzarek would play keyboard bass. For their studio work, the band recruited a number of musicians to handle bass duties. One of these was blues-rocker Lonnie Mack, whose aggressive guitar style influenced Jeff Beck and Stevie Ray Vaughan, among many others. Another was Harvey Brooks, who also played on Bob Dylan's seminal rock album *Highway 61 Revisited* (1965).

CREAM

Most bands would seem hubristic if they called themselves something like "Cream" (as in "cream of the crop"). This 60s power trio, on the other hand, was just being honest. People in the British music scene had already recognized guitarist Eric Clapton, bassist Jack Bruce, and drummer Ginger Baker as stellar musicians before they formed Cream. On hit albums like *Disraeli*

Gears (1967) and *Wheels of Fire* (1968), they left no doubt by mixing hard-rocking singles like "Sunshine of Your Love" and "White Room" with extended jams.

It wasn't easy being Cream, though. Even before the group formed, there were considerable tensions between Bruce and Baker. The two musicians had already played together in the Graham Bond Organization. During that time, they'd fight during shows and mess with each other's instruments. At one point, Baker even threatened Bruce with a knife. All things considered, it's a miracle that Cream even made one album, let alone the first double album to go platinum (i.e. *Wheels of Fire*).

JANIS JOPLIN

When Janis Joplin was attending the University of Texas at Austin, the campus newspaper did a story on her. The headline for the article was, "She Dares to Be Different."

They weren't whistling Dixie. In concert and on recordings like "Piece of My Heart" and "Ball and Chain," Joplin's raw, soulful singing stunned critics and audiences alike. Critic Richard Goldstein called her "the most staggering leading woman in rock." She also inspired female artists ranging from Stevie Nicks to Pink.

Joplin got respect from the soul and R&B artists she admired too. Etta James once called her "an angel who came and paved a road white chicks hadn't walked before. I began feeling proud to be her role model." Joplin also got to sing a duet with Tina Turner at Madison Square Garden in 1969 (photographer Amalie R.

Rothschild took a picture of this performance, which she gave as a gift to President Bill Clinton in 2000).

SLY AND THE FAMILY STONE

Perhaps no music captures the wildness and optimism of the 60s counterculture quite like the psychedelic soul of Sly and the Family Stone does. Songs like "Dance to the Music," "I Want to Take You Higher," and "Everyday People" created a vision of a better tomorrow for all races, genders, and classes. The band's lineup reflected this vision as well—in the Rock and Roll Hall of Fame's words, they were "rock's first integrated, multi-gender band."

Unfortunately, that vision couldn't hold up under the pressures of fame, drug abuse, and conflicts between band members. The Black Panthers told bandleader Sly Stone to replace the white members of the group with black musicians (he didn't, but they ended up leaving eventually anyway). Stone also had gangsters serve as his bodyguards, which helped alienate him from his bandmates. His life and career deteriorated to the point where the *New York Post* reported in 2011 that he was living in a camper in Crenshaw, California.

Still, the Family Stone's music endures. Artists like Michael Jackson, George Clinton, Prince, and the Black Eyed Peas have drawn inspiration from their work.

GRAM PARSONS

Remember that dictionary of yours that should have a picture of the Byrds under "folk-rock"? It should have a picture of Gram Parsons under "country rock" too. Both as a solo artist and a member of groups like the Byrds and the Flying Burrito Brothers, Parsons' self-proclaimed "cosmic American music" helped pave the way for acts ranging from the Eagles (whose lineup featured former Flying Burrito Brothers member Bernie Leadon) to Wilco and Ryan Adams.

Parsons' influence doesn't stop there. He befriended Rolling Stones guitarist Keith Richards and taught him a lot about country music (Parsons stayed in France with Richards while the Stones were recording their 1972 masterpiece *Exile on Main St.*). He also helped country star Emmylou Harris early in her career. Harris sings harmony on Parsons' solo albums *GP* (1973) and *Grievous Angel* (1974). After Parsons died, she recruited members of his band to form her backing group the Hot Band. Harris has covered his songs and referenced him in her own lyrics numerous times over the years.

MC5

Along with their counterparts in the Stooges, the Detroit hard rock group MC5 was about as far as you could get from the mellow, "peace and love" hippie ideal. How far is that, you ask? For one thing, they were the only group to play outside the infamous 1968 Democratic convention in Chicago, where 27,000 local, state, and federal officers beat and fired tear gas at anti-Vietnam war protesters.

The MC5's music was plenty violent in itself too. Their anarchic debut album *Kick Out the Jams* (1969)—recorded live at the Grande Ballroom over two nights—is a recognized precursor for punk rock. Although the group would record two more albums and inspire many rock artists that followed them, bassist Michael Davis saw *Kick Out the Jams* as "the end of the band."

"We were like Play-Doh before that, and then we were an actual form after it, and we were expected to be like that from then on," he told *Uncut* in 2012.

THE VELVET UNDERGROUND

In a 1982 interview, British musician Brian Eno recalled that Lou Reed, the Velvet Underground's lead singer and songwriter, told him that *The Velvet Underground and Nico* (1967) only sold 30,000 copies in its first five years. "I think everyone who bought one of those 30,000 copies started a band!" Eno quipped.

He might have been right. The Velvet Underground's mix of arty drones and distortion, pop songcraft, and provocative lyrical content was a major influence on punk, new wave, post-punk, and alternative rock. Nirvana covered their song "Here She Comes Now" on a single in 1991 (the other side featured the Melvins' take on the Velvet Underground's "Venus in Furs").

The Velvet Underground's work even had an impact on international politics. The band's songs inspired members of the 1989 "Velvet Revolution," which overthrew Communist rule in Czechoslovakia. When Czech president Vaclav Havel visited the White House in 1998, he specifically requested that Lou Reed perform there.

RANDOM FUN FACTS

1. Jimi Hendrix may have been a great guitarist, but he didn't always excel in other things. He enlisted in the US Army in 1961 but was discharged the following year for unsuitability. His brief stint in the Army wasn't a total waste, though. He became friends with Billy Cox, who would later play bass in Hendrix's Band of Gypsys.

2. One of the odder releases in Roger McGuinn's post-Byrds career is his album *Live from Mars* (1996). The music itself isn't strange—it's a mixture of songs that inspired him and his old hits. But why on Earth does it have the cast of the cult TV show *Mystery Science Theater 3000* on the cover? And why does it have liner notes by show character Tom Servo? McGuinn explained it this way in a 1996 interview: "The idea was to give the album a whimsical spin to go with the title." Um, okay then...

3. Although they sang a lot about surfing, only one member of the Beach Boys actually surfed: Dennis Wilson. In addition to singing and playing drums, Dennis starred in the cult classic film *Two-Lane Blacktop* (1971) and was friends (very briefly) with mass murderer Charles Manson.

4. After playing the 1965 Newport Folk Festival, Bob Dylan left his Fender Stratocaster guitar on a plane. The plane's

pilot and his family kept it for more than four decades before bringing it out in a 2012 episode of the PBS TV series *History Detectives*. Alt-country musician Jason Isbell played the guitar at the 2015 Newport Folk Festival during a tribute to Dylan's '65 set.

5. A 19-year-old Bruce Springsteen saw Janis Joplin perform at the Asbury Park Convention Hall in 1969. She spotted him and liked what she saw, but Springsteen got too nervous and left the show before she could approach him.

6. Even at an early age, Paul McCartney had songwriting down. He wrote "When I'm Sixty-Four," which shows up on The Beatles' landmark album *Sgt. Pepper's Lonely Hearts Club Band* (1967), when he was only 16. It was one of the first songs he wrote too. Talk about getting off to a good start!

7. One legendary part of James Brown's live shows was the so-called "cape act." Brown would pretend to be too exhausted to continue the show but come back to life as soon as someone tried to put a cape on him and lead him offstage. According to Brown's valet Danny Ray, this famous bit of stagecraft developed by accident: "I used to catch him coming off singing ['Please Please Please'] and he'd just be drenched in sweat, and one thing I was supposed to do was hand him a towel. That's all it was."

8. Before starting the Kinks, the Davies brothers formed a band called the Ray Davies Quartet. For a brief period, the

lead singer for the group was future rock star Rod Stewart.

9. The Rolling Stones got their name pretty much by accident. According to Keith Richards, guitarist Brian Jones came up with it while talking with *Jazz News* on the phone. When the publication asked for the band's name, Jones looked at a Muddy Waters LP lying at his feet, which had the song "Rollin' Stone" on it.

10. No two groups could seem more different than quintessential hippies the Grateful Dead and punk godfathers the Velvet Underground. But both bands went by the same name early in their careers: The Warlocks.

11. Before playing with Rick James and Buffalo Springfield, Bruce Palmer played with the Canadian rock group Jack London & the Sparrows. After Palmer left, other members of the Sparrows formed Steppenwolf, which is best known for the classic rock anthem "Born to Be Wild."

12. According to *Billboard*, Creedence Clearwater Revival holds the record for "Artists who most often reached No. 2 but were unable to top the Hot 100." They scored five No. 2 singles while runners-up Blood, Sweat & Tears, and En Vogue each scored three.

13. The Yardbirds' name is a reference to jazz saxophonist Charlie Parker.

14. John Entwistle's astonishingly fluid, melodic basslines were one of the defining characteristics of the Who's sound. He

wasn't able to buy a bass at first, so he built one of his own.

15. Jim Morrison briefly dated cult Los Angeles author Eve Babitz, who tried to persuade him not to call his band "The Doors" ("I mean, [Aldous Huxley's] *The Doors of Perception*... what an Ojaigeeky-too-L.A.-pottery-glazer kind of uncool idea," she once wrote). Babitz was also the inspiration for the Doors' song "L.A. Woman."

TEST YOURSELF – QUESTIONS AND ANSWERS

1. The Rolling Stones' Keith Richards had a brief romance with which American girl group singer?

A) Diana Ross

B) Ronnie Spector

C) Martha Reeves

2. Which 60s soul singer wrote the Janis Joplin-covered song "Get It While You Can?"

A) Howard Tate

B) Clarence Reid

C) Otis Redding

3. Which English rock guitarist became a superstar in the 70s after playing with Humble Pie in the late 60s?

A) Eric Clapton

B) Robin Trower

C) Peter Frampton

4. Cream drummer Ginger Baker played with which groundbreaking African musician?

A) King Sunny Ade

B) Fela Kuti

C) Youssou N'Dour

5. Which country star did Gram Parsons try to get to produce his first solo album?

A) Johnny Cash

B) George Jones

C) Merle Haggard

ANSWERS

1. B
2. A
3. C
4. B
5. C

CHAPTER TWO

ARTISTS OF THE 70S

In the 1970s, the hope and joy of the 60s gave way to cynicism and disillusionment. Rock music reflected this shift in such albums as Sly and the Family Stone's *There's a Riot Goin' On* (1971), Funkadelic's *Maggot Brain* (1971), the Rolling Stones' *Exile on Main St.* (1972), Pink Floyd's *Dark Side of the Moon* (1973), and Neil Young's *On the Beach* (1974). Perhaps that made the decade the perfect time for the ascendance of sinister heavy metal groups like Black Sabbath.

The 70s weren't all doom and gloom, though. From a series of vibrant masterpieces from artists like Van Morrison and Stevie Wonder to the emergence of power pop, reggae, disco, and punk, there was plenty of music to raise the spirits and keep the faith alive. Here's some info on a few of the artists who provided the soundtrack for the decade.

NEIL YOUNG

"It's better to burn out than to fade away," Neil Young sang on the album *Rust Never Sleeps* (1979). Ironically, the Canadian singer-songwriter was still burning bright when so many of his peers had done one or the other.

After spending three years in Buffalo Springfield and releasing two solo albums in the 60s, Young would emerge in the 70s as one of rock and roll's premier artists. He released music ranging from the wistful folk and country of *After the Gold Rush* (1970), *Harvest* (1972), and *Comes a Time* (1978) to the drugged-out menace of *Tonight's the Night* (1975) and the hypnotic guitar workouts of *Zuma* (1975). In the process, he helped set precedence for 90s alt-country groups like Uncle Tupelo and the Old '97s and earned a reputation as the "Godfather of Grunge."

Young has made an impact outside of music as well. Along with Willie Nelson and John Cougar Mellencamp, he organized Farm Aid, which provides support to family farms across America. The first Farm Aid concert in 1985 raised more than $9 million for farmers. Young and his ex-wife Pegi also organized the Bridge School Concerts, which help raise money to develop technology for children with disabilities.

Young has even influenced the world of toy trains and railroads. He bought part of the toy train company Lionel, LLC in the 90s and helped design a control system for their trains. Not only that, he's listed as co-inventor on several U.S. patents involving model trains. At least he'll have something to fall back on in case music doesn't work out.

VAN MORRISON

After scoring hits both with the Irish R&B band Them and as a solo artist in the 60s, Van Morrison achieved even greater acclaim in the 70s. On classic albums like *Moondance* (1970),

His Band and the Street Choir (1970), and *Tupelo Honey* (1971), he blended together soul music, rock, jazz, Celtic folk, and cryptic, stream-of-consciousness poetry. He scored hits like "Domino" and "Wild Night" and received tremendous praise from critics like Lester Bangs and Greil Marcus, who called him "visionary in the strongest sense of the word." He would also influence rock artists ranging from Bruce Springsteen and Thin Lizzy's Phil Lynott to U2, Nick Cave, and Jeff Buckley.

Like plenty of artistic geniuses, Morrison has earned a reputation for being difficult. He started suffering from stage fright as his crowds got larger in the 70s. When he performed with the Band for their 1976 farewell concert, promoter Harvey Goldsmith said that he "literally had to kick him out there." When Morrison was inducted into the Rock and Roll Hall of Fame in 1993, he earned the dubious distinction of being the first living artist that didn't attend his own ceremony.

DAVID BOWIE

David Bowie's name is practically synonymous with artistic reinvention. Born David Robert Jones in 1947, he first gained mainstream attention with his 1969 hit song "Space Oddity." Over the course of the 70s, Bowie released hit albums like *The Rise and Fall of Ziggy Stardust and the Spiders from Mars* (1972) and *Diamond Dogs* (1974) and switched between glam rock, soul, funk, disco, and experimental electronica. He also gave support to his influences, producing *Transformer* (1972) for ex-Velvet Underground frontman Lou Reed and *The Idiot* (1977) and *Lust for Life* (1977) for Iggy Pop (he also produced *Raw Power* (1973) for Pop's old band the Stooges).

For most artists, these achievements would be enough. But Bowie accomplished much more. His elaborately theatrical live shows paved the way for the arena extravaganzas of Madonna, Lady Gaga, Beyoncé, and many other pop artists. His androgynous, explicitly gay Ziggy Stardust persona made sexual identity a subject for pop culture. When Bowie died in 2016, *The Guardian* called him "the most important and influential artist since the Beatles."

Considering the indelible mark that he made on rock music and culture in general, it's amazing to think that Bowie's showbiz career almost ended before it really began. Back in 1967, Bowie strongly considered devoting his life to Buddhism. In his own words, "I was within a month of having my head shaved, taking my vows, and becoming a monk." When he consulted a Buddhist teacher, however, the monk advised Bowie to keep making music.

LED ZEPPELIN

Rising from the ashes of the 60s blues-rock group the Yardbirds, Led Zeppelin released a series of albums in the late 60s and 70s that went a long way towards setting the template for heavy metal. Their massive riffs, lumbering rhythms, and banshee vocals influenced a wide variety of artists, including Deep Purple, Soundgarden, the White Stripes, and even Lady Gaga, who told the BBC in 2009 that she used to sing in a Led Zeppelin cover band.

In their prime, Led Zeppelin became almost as well known for stories of their debauched antics as for their music. For instance, there's the story of drummer John Bonham riding a motorcycle around a floor of the Continental Hyatt House (nicknamed "The Riot House") in Los Angeles. There's also the sexual relationship that guitarist Jimmy Page carried on with Lori Maddux, a groupie who was only 15 at the time. In a 2015 interview for Thrillist, Maddux said she didn't feel exploited—she remembered Page asking her mom for permission to be with her. Still, the affair led to some tense situations—Maddux also recalled being told to leave a hotel when the band had $200,000 stolen from them in New York and the FBI was investigating.

JONI MITCHELL

Although she gained recognition in the 60s for songs like "Both Sides Now" and "Chelsea Morning," Joni Mitchell's 70s work established her as a major creative force. While *Blue* (1971) stunned audiences and critics with its detailed, confessional lyrics, albums like *For the Roses* (1972), *Court and Spark* (1974), and *Hejira* (1976) shifted between folk, jazz, pop, and rock with impressive ease. These records made Mitchell, in author David Shumway's words, "the first woman in popular music to be recognized as an artist in the full sense of that term." Artists from Madonna to Mikael Akerfeldt from the Swedish progressive death metal band Opeth have cited her as a crucial inspiration.

One unique aspect of Mitchell's music is her frequent use of alternative guitar tunings. Mitchell contracted polio as a child, which affected her ability to play guitar in the standard EADGBE tuning. As a result of this, she began developing her own. Over the years, she has written songs in approximately 50 different tunings.

STEVIE WONDER

Well before the 1970s, Stevie Wonder had secured a place in the history of American popular music. He signed to Motown's Tamla label in 1961 at age 11 and scored his first hit record when he was only 13 ("Fingertips" reached #1 on Billboard's Pop Singles chart in 1963). He also wrote and recorded such 60s hits as "Uptight (Everything's Alright)" and "I Was Made to Love Her."

However, it was in the 70s that Wonder's astonishing talent fully matured. A 1972 tour with the Rolling Stones helped him reach a larger audience. After that, albums like *Talking Book* (1972), *Innervisions* (1973), and *Songs in the Key of Life* (1976) found Wonder tackling socio-political themes while still delivering hit tunes. Not only that, he made most of this great music all by himself. On *Innervisions*, for example, he plays all the instruments on seven of the album's nine songs.

Wonder made an impact outside of music too. In the late 70s and early 80s, he helped galvanize the effort to make Martin Luther King Jr.'s birthday a national holiday in the United States.

BLACK SABBATH

If Led Zeppelin laid the foundations for heavy metal, Black Sabbath filled in the main floor. Founded in Birmingham, England, in 1968, the band made a string of albums in the 70s that combined oozing rhythms, ominous riffs and lyrics about demons, wizards, robots, and other sinister subjects. Practically every metal band worth talking about has cited Sabbath as an influence, including Judas Priest, Iron Maiden, Slayer, and Metallica. Lamb of God drummer Chris Adler might have put it best: "If anybody who plays heavy metal says that they weren't influenced by Black Sabbath's music, then I think that they're lying to you."

Plenty of people probably know that the band took their name from the 1963 Boris Karloff horror film of the same title. However, not as many people may know that their songs drew inspiration from the stories of Dennis Wheatley, an English thriller writer whose work often touched on occult and supernatural subjects. Wheatley's stories were also adapted into Hammer horror movies and helped inspire Ian Fleming's James Bond novels.

BIG STAR

Although their prime only lasted from 1971 to 1974, Big Star would cast a long shadow over the rock bands that followed them. Their eccentric, brooding take on British Invasion-era rock has earned them a reputation as, in music writer Jason Ankeny's words, "the quintessential American power pop band." Fans of the TV sitcom *That '70s Show* will know Cheap Trick's cover of Big Star's song "In the Street," which played over the show's opening credits. Jason Isbell, Wilco, Whiskeytown, and the Bangles have all covered the group's songs as well. In addition to those bands, REM, the Replacements (whose song "Alex Chilton" paid tribute to the group's lead singer and songwriter) and even Paul Stanley from Kiss have cited Big Star as an inspiration.

Before teaming up with the other members of Big Star, Alex Chilton was the lead singer of the blue-eyed soul group the Box Tops, which scored a #1 Billboard Hot 100 hit with "The Letter" in 1967. After that group broke up, jazz-rock group Blood, Sweat & Tears invited Chilton to sing for their band, but he passed on their offer. Who knows what could've happened if he hadn't? He could've been a big star, possibly, but he wouldn't have been Big Star.

PINK FLOYD

If Pink Floyd had broken up after Syd Barrett—the group's original lead singer and songwriter—got dropped from the lineup in 1967, they might be little more than a footnote in rock history today. But with bassist Roger Waters assuming the role of main creative force, the progressive rock band became one of the most successful groups of all time. Hit albums like *The Dark Side of the Moon* (1973), *Wish You Were Here* (1975), and *The Wall* (1979) would inspire groups like Radiohead, Nine Inch Nails, and Smashing Pumpkins.

Pink Floyd is so well known for their songs' themes of alienation and social oppression that their connection to one of the funniest films of all time may surprise people. The band provided financial support for the filming of the 1975 movie *Monty Python and the Holy Grail* along with Led Zeppelin, Jethro Tull, Andrew Lloyd Webber, and other people in the music industry. They got their investment back and then some: Producer John Goldstone told the *Chicago Tribune* in 2009 that *Holy Grail*'s investors "had seen a 6,000 percent return on their money."

LYNYRD SKYNYRD

The Allman Brothers Band may have invented what we think of as southern rock, but no group exemplified the genre better than Lynyrd Skynyrd. Lead singer and lyricist Ronnie Van Zant formed the band in 1964 along with guitarists Allen Collins and Gary Rossington, drummer Bob Burns, and bassist Larry Junstrom. They changed their band's name several times before settling on Lynyrd Skynyrd, a joke on their high school P.E. teacher Leonard Skinner.

Skynyrd is best known today for the epic ballad (and tiresome live show joke) "Free Bird" and the twangy anthem "Sweet Home Alabama," the latter of which was written partly in response to Neil Young's scathing protest songs "Southern Man" and "Alabama." Ironically, Young loved the song and the band. He even went so far as to offer Skynyrd his songs "Powderfinger" and "Sedan Delivery," which later turned up on his album *Rust Never Sleeps* (1979).

The respect was mutual: The cover photograph of Skynyrd's album *Street Survivors* (1977) shows Ronnie Van Zant wearing a Neil Young t-shirt.

GEORGE CLINTON AND PARLIAMENT/FUNKADELIC

In the 70s, George Clinton went from being a staff songwriter for Motown and doo-wop group leader to an audaciously irreverent sci-fi funk ringleader. With the funk-centric group Parliament and the more rock-oriented Funkadelic (both of which originally featured the same members), Clinton blended the rhythmic innovations of James Brown and Sly Stone with Jimi Hendrix-esque psychedelic guitar and clever vocal arrangements. His work would prove as big an influence on hip-hop as James Brown's.

Indeed, the connection between Clinton and Brown goes much deeper than simple artistic inspiration. Clinton recruited several of Brown's key collaborators, including bassist Bootsy Collins, guitarist Catfish Collins, saxophonist Maceo Parker, and trombonist Fred Wesley (who also handled arrangements for—and even wrote —some of Brown's classic tracks).

JIMMY CLIFF

Desmond Dekker helped lead the way in the 1960s with singles like "007 (Shanty Town)" and "Israelites," but two early 70s releases are credited with breaking reggae music out of Jamaica and giving it a worldwide audience. One was the Wailers' classic album *Catch a Fire* (1972). The other was the soundtrack for the 1972 film *The Harder They Come*, which prominently featured songs by Jimmy Cliff (who also starred in the movie).

In a way, Cliff played a key role in making reggae music's international popularity possible. In 1961, Cliff met producer and business owner Leslie Kong. He was only 12 or 13 at the time, but his talent impressed Kong so much that the older man launched his own label to record Cliff's music. Soon after that, Cliff introduced Bob Marley to Kong, who recorded the future superstar's very first single. Kong went on to record such leading reggae acts as Toots and the Maytals and Desmond Dekker (including the songs "007" and "Israelites").

Ironically, Bob Marley and the Wailers' growing success created a stumbling block in Cliff's career. When the band started to take off, Island Records turned their focus away from him to Marley. Still, Cliff's music endures—none other than Bob Dylan called Cliff's song "Vietnam" the best protest song he'd ever heard.

THE RUNAWAYS

The Runaways were a bit like Buffalo Springfield in that their members went on to far greater success after they split up. The similarities pretty much stop there, though. Forming in Los Angeles in 1975 under the guidance of oddball producer Kim Fowley, the all-female Runaways split the difference between punk and heavy metal. Their in-your-face attitude and no-nonsense music inspired female-fronted bands to rock out, including Hole, Bikini Kill, and White Lung.

After the Runaways broke up in 1979, guitarists Joan Jett and Lita Ford went on to highly successful solo careers. Bassist Micki Steele played with pop-rock group the Bangles, which scored such hits as "Walk Like an Egyptian" and "Manic Monday" in the 1980s. Lead singer Cherie Currie has released music as a solo artist and acted in movies. However, Currie's biggest passion is something even edgier than rock and roll—chainsaw carving!

NEW YORK DOLLS

In 2011, the glam metal bands Mötley Crue and Poison embarked on a summer tour. The opener on this tour was a group called the New York Dolls.

Anyone who knew their punk and hard rock history could have seen the irony of this arrangement. With their flamboyant, androgynous fashion sense and raucous, devilishly playful songs like "Personality Crisis," "Trash," and "Lookin' for a Kiss," the New York Dolls essentially wrote the glam metal playbook. But their impact on rock runs even deeper—members of the Ramones, the Clash, and the Sex Pistols have all cited the Dolls as a major inspiration. So has British singer-songwriter Morrissey, who organized a Dolls reunion at London's

Meltdown Festival in 2004.

Even if you've never seen or heard the Dolls, you may know lead singer David Johansen. He scored a hit in 1987 with a cover of the calypso song "Hot Hot Hot," which he released under the pseudonym Buster Poindexter. Johansen also appeared as the cab-driving Ghost of Christmas Past in the 1988 film *Scrooged*.

CHIC

Although dance hits like "Le Freak," "Good Times," and "Dance, Dance, Dance (Yowsah, Yowsah, Yowsah)" may make the 'disco sucks' crowd turn up their noses, Chic made a lot of great music in the 70s. They helped make a lot of classic rock and pop possible too. Queen's "Another One Bites the Dust," Blondie's "Rapture," The Sugarhill Gang's "Rapper's Delight," and Daft Punk's "Around the World" all sampled or drew inspiration from Chic's song "Good Times."

Chic's masterminds, guitarist Nile Rodgers and bassist Bernard Edwards, played a more direct role in other great records. Edwards produced bestselling albums by Robert Palmer and Rod Stewart in the 1980s. Rodgers' production credits are even more impressive. They include such chart-topping albums as Diana Ross' *Diana* (1980), David Bowie's *Let's Dance* (1983), Madonna's *Like a Virgin* (1984), and the B-52s' *Cosmic Thing* (1989). More recently, Rodgers contributed his signature chicken-scratch guitar style to Daft Punk's hit singles "Get Lucky" and "Lose Yourself to Dance."

Even some of Chic's hired hands hit it big. R&B singer Luther Vandross sang backup vocals for the band before becoming a solo star in the 1980s.

TELEVISION

Television never became as popular as their peers in Blondie and the Talking Heads, but they still made their mark and then some. They were the first band connected to the New York punk scene to play the now-legendary venue CBGB's. Their first album *Marquee Moon* (1977) is considered one of the greatest and most influential rock records of the 1970's. Television's elegant yet fiery brand of guitar rock influenced many groups that followed them, including U2, the Pixies, Sonic Youth, REM, and Echo and the Bunnymen.

Although he quit the band well before they recorded *Marquee Moon*, original bassist Richard Hell was just as influential if not more so. Sex Pistols manager Malcolm McLaren ripped off Hell's spiky hair and torn, safety-pinned clothes, making them part of the dominant style of the UK punk scene. Hell's nihilistic, thrill-seeking persona helped define the stereotypical punk attitude as well.

THE RAMONES

Except for the Sex Pistols (maybe), no other punk band was more influential than the Ramones. Forming in 1974, the band's loud, fast, funny, three/four-chord songs set the template for punk rock and hardcore. Music historian Jon Savage called their debut album *Ramones* (1976) "one of the few records that changed pop forever." Their leather jackets, torn jeans, and sneakers were equally influential on the punk "look."

Ironically, the Ramones didn't think of themselves as a revolutionary band. "We thought we were a bubblegum band," lead singer Joey Ramone admitted in an interview. Their anthem "Blitzkrieg Bop" was originally intended to emulate songs like "Saturday Night" by the Scottish pop band Bay City Rollers. Funny how things turn out!

THE SEX PISTOLS

"The Pistols had to come in and blow everything away," Clash frontman Joe Strummer once said. "They were that stun grenade into the room before the door could go."

Indeed, they were. The Sex Pistols' thunderous anthems and confrontational, take-no-prisoners attitude more or less kick-started the entire UK punk scene. The Clash, Siouxsie and the Banshees, and Joy Division were among the many groups inspired by the Pistols. In the late 70s, they became infamous for incidents like their curse-filled interview with Bill Grundy on Thames Television's *Today* program. Conservative politician Bernard Brook-Partridge went so far as to call them "the antithesis of humankind."

Although lead singer Johnny Rotten and bassist Sid Vicious became the most iconic members of the group, the Sex Pistols would never have come together without guitarist Steve Jones.

In 1972, Jones formed the Strand with drummer Paul Cook and guitarist Wally Nightingale. It was Jones who convinced Malcolm McLaren to manage the group. Eventually, the band dropped Nightingale, recruited Rotten and bassist Glen Matlock, and changed their name to the Sex Pistols.

It didn't take long for anarchy to ensue. At their very first gig, the Pistols got the plugs pulled on their instruments and scuffled with the headlining band.

THE CLASH

In the late 70s, CBS ran ads calling the Clash "the only band that matters." The tagline ran contrary to the group's egalitarian ideals, but today, lots of people would agree.

Founded in 1976, the Clash's radical left-wing politics gave punk rockers an alternative to the nihilistic, "No Future" ethos of the Sex Pistols. On albums like *London Calling* (1979/1980) and *Sandinista!* (1981), they experimented with reggae, funk, hip-hop, rockabilly, and other musical styles. A broad range of artists have drawn inspiration from the Clash over the years, including U2, Billy Bragg, Green Day, Rage Against the Machine, and M.I.A.

Given his strong sympathy for the working class, lead singer Joe Strummer's privileged background may surprise some people. Born John Graham Mellor, Strummer's father Ronald was a British diplomat. Strummer traveled with his family around the world until he was nine, when his parents sent him and his brother David to boarding school. The Mellors weren't exactly posh, though. Clash biographer Pat Gilbert wrote that "his father's work meant little more than constant upheaval and an ever-shifting backdrop of tastes, smells, languages, and climates." Actually, that's not a bad start for the guy who would write "White Riot" and "Tommy Gun."

JOY DIVISION

Joy Division only put out two studio albums and a handful of singles, but artists are still drawing inspiration from their music. The band formed in Manchester in 1976 after guitarist Bernard Sumner and bassist Peter Hook saw the Sex Pistols perform. Frontman Ian Curtis' tortured lyrics and the band's melodic basslines, spare guitar lines, and propulsive drums established them as one of the first post-punk and proto-gothic rock groups. After Curtis committed suicide in 1980, the band changed their name to New Order and became one of the most influential groups of the 80s.

Songs like "She's Lost Control," "Transmission," and "Love Will Tear Us Apart" earned Joy Division a devoted fan base. After Curtis' death, someone painted the words "Ian Curtis Lives" on a wall on Wallace Street in Wellington, New Zealand. These words have been painted over several times over the years, but they always reappear (though at some point, the inscription apparently changed to "Ian Curtis RIP"). Today, this wall is known among Wellington residents as the "Ian Curtis Wall."

RANDOM FUN FACTS

1. Led Zeppelin's name came from a joke made by John Entwistle and Keith Moon from the Who. Originally, Jimmy Page was thinking about forming a supergroup with Entwistle, Moon, and guitarist Jeff Beck. Entwistle and Moon quipped that a group with both Page and Beck in it would go down like a "lead balloon" (i.e. would be a disaster).

2. Stevie Wonder had originally intended to give his smash hit song "Superstition" to guitarist Jeff Beck to release first. The two musicians had worked together to create the first demo for the song (Beck came up with its drum beat). Motown sensed that "Superstition" would be extremely popular, however, which led to Wonder's version coming out before Beck's (it didn't help that problems with Beck's band prevented the release of his version until 1973).

3. Black Sabbath guitarist Tony Iommi briefly left the band in December 1968 to join English rock band Jethro Tull. He didn't stay with them very long, however—he went back to Black Sabbath (then called Earth) in January 1969.

4. When Neil Young performed at the Band's 1976 farewell concert, he had a piece of cocaine hanging from his nose. Filmmaker Martin Scorsese recorded the show for the film

The Last Waltz (1978), and Young's manager Elliot Roberts had to beg him to edit out the lump.

5. Syd Barrett may have been kicked out of Pink Floyd before their tremendous success in the 70s, but he still made his mark on rock music. Paul McCartney, David Bowie, and T. Rex's Marc Bolan all cited him as an inspiration.

6. Bassist Larry Junstrom may have left Lynyrd Skynyrd in 1971, but he still "kept it in the family." He later joined the rock band .38 Special, which was led by Ronnie Van Zant's younger brother Donnie.

7. David Bowie's career wasn't without missteps or regrettable moments. In the mid 70s, he expressed an admiration for fascism in a series of interviews. In one such interview, he said, "I think Britain could benefit from a fascist leader. After all, fascism is really nationalism." *NME* also published a photo in which Bowie allegedly gave a "sieg heil" salute to a crowd of people. Bowie strongly denied doing this—he claimed he was just waving—and later blamed his comments on his abuse of cocaine and other substances.

8. Led Zeppelin's song "Going to California" is allegedly about Joni Mitchell.

9. One crucial element of Parliament-Funkadelic's sound is the synthesizer work of Bernie Worrell. A child prodigy, Worrell started taking classical piano lessons at age 3 and wrote a concerto at age 8. Also, he was the second musician

to own an original Moog synthesizer.

10. On top of her work with the Runaways and as a solo artist, Joan Jett has also produced releases by seminal hardcore punk band the Germs (the 1979 album *GI*) and original riot grrl band Bikini Kill (a 7" single of their anthem "Rebel Girl").

11. In addition to his music, Belfast-born Van Morrison has helped promote tourism in Northern Ireland. In recognition of these achievements, he was knighted by Prince Charles of Wales in 2016. "For 53 years, I've been in the business— that's not bad for a blue-eyed soul singer from east Belfast," Morrison told *The Telegraph*.

12. When the Ramones started playing in the mid-to-late 70s, they were seen as an antidote to the overblown arena excess of groups like Led Zeppelin. Ironically, guitarist Johnny Ramone once cited Jimmy Page as a major inspiration. "He's probably the greatest guitarist who ever lived," Ramone told interviewer Robert Jones.

13. In 1972, drummer Marc Bell auditioned for the New York Dolls. He didn't make the cut, but he later played drums on Richard Hell's classic punk album *Blank Generation* (1977). He also played for 14 years with the Ramones as Marky Ramone.

14. The song "Fascination" from David Bowie's album *Young Americans* (1975) was co-written by Bowie and Luther Vandross. Vandross also sang backup for Bowie on a late

1974 tour.

15. The Sex Pistols played their first live concert on November 6, 1975. They opened for the pub rock group Bazooka Joe, which featured bassist Stuart Goddard. Goddard quit the band soon after that show and went on to great success as Adam Ant.

TEST YOURSELF – QUESTIONS AND ANSWERS

1. Which guitarist played on an alternate version of the Rolling Stones' hit 1971 song "Brown Sugar?"

A) Brian Jones

B) Eric Clapton

C) Pete Townshend

2. Lynyrd Skynyrd's 1974 song "Sweet Home Alabama" name-checks which legendary band of session musicians?

A) The Swampers

B) The M.G.'s

C) The Funk Brothers

3. Which rock superstar started covering Jimmy Cliff's 1970s song "Trapped" in the 80s?

A) David Bowie

B) Bono from U2

C) Bruce Springsteen

4. Which group did Richard Hell form with Johnny Thunders and Jerry Nolan from the New York Dolls?

A) The Heartbreakers

B) The Voidoids

C) Dim Stars

5. The Ramones took their name from which rock star's old pseudonym?

A) Ray Davies

B) John Lennon

C) Paul McCartney

ANSWERS

1. B
2. A
3. C
4. A
5. C

CHAPTER THREE

ARTISTS OF THE 80S

The 1980s saw their share of social and political upheaval, but they also saw much more than their share of great music. It came in all kinds of genres too—arena rock, punk, post-punk, pop, funk, heavy metal, and hip-hop, to name just a few. Here are some tidbits on the biggest artists of the 80s.

MICHAEL JACKSON

Michael Jackson had hit singles both as a solo artist and with the Jackson 5 in the 1970s. It was in the 80s, however, that he truly became the "King of Pop."

Jackson had joined forces with ace arranger and producer Quincy Jones to make *Off the Wall* (1979), which reached number three on the *Billboard* 200 and earned Jackson a Grammy and two American Music Awards. Jackson also got to make music industry history in 1980 by getting a whopping 37% of the profits for album sales, the highest royalty rate for any recording artist.

In spite of these achievements, Jackson and Jones' next collaboration was the real mind-blower. Featuring seven singles that made the *Billboard* Hot 100's top 10, *Thriller* (1982) became the bestselling album of all time in the US in 1983. Having sold

65 million copies and counting, it is considered the all-time bestselling album in the world today. Jackson's career had numerous controversies and strange moments in the years that followed, but the power and popularity of his music remains undiminished.

Even the Library of Congress has acknowledged the importance of Jackson's work. The 14-minute film for his hit song "Thriller" is the only music video to be included in the Library's National Film Registry.

PRINCE

Prince Rogers Nelson released two well-received albums in the late 70s, but the work he put out in the 80s made him a superstar. Beginning with the polymorphously perverse *Dirty Mind* (1980), Prince released a string of hit albums that fused funk, soul, rock, and synth-pop. These included *1999* (1982), *Purple Rain* (1984), and *Sign O' the Times* (1987). Critics have praised both his ability to upend racial and gender stereotypes and his astonishing musical versatility—he played almost all the parts on his first five albums (the credits for his 1978 debut album list 27 instruments that he played).

As prolific and generous as Prince could be with his music—he'd originally intended the double album *Sign O' the Times* to be a triple album—he could get quite stingy when it came to online photos and videos of him. In 2013, the international non-profit Electronic Frontier Foundation gave him the "Raspberry Beret Lifetime Aggrievement Award" for, in their words, "extraordinary abuses of the [Digital Millennium Copyright Act's] takedown process in the name of silencing speech." Well, if you were as talented as Prince, maybe you'd get protective too.

BRUCE SPRINGSTEEN

The release of the classic album *Born to Run* (1975) had made Bruce Springsteen a rock star, but *Born in the USA* (1984) made him a bona fide American icon. Featuring seven top-10 hits—including the oft-misinterpreted title track—the album was a worldwide hit and has become one of the bestselling albums of all time. He is widely beloved today for his powerful live shows and his songs' trenchant, rousing depictions of working-class struggles.

From a young age, people recognized Springsteen's talent and charisma. When he was just 19, he and his band Child (later called Steel Mill) was managing to build a dedicated following along the East Coast. In fact, Child was even invited to play Woodstock! Manager Carl "Tinker" West turned the offer down, though—the band already had a show booked. Naturally, West kicked himself for making that decision later.

MADONNA

When David Bowie was inducted into the Rock and Roll Hall of Fame in 1996, Madonna gave the induction speech. In it, she recalled seeing Bowie in concert as a teenager.

"I don't think that I breathed for two hours," she said. "It was the most amazing show that I'd ever seen, not just because the music was great, but because it was great theater."

Lots of people would say the same of Madonna herself. Like Bowie, she combined irresistible songs like "Material Girl," "Like a Virgin," "Like a Prayer" (which features Prince on guitar), and "Express Yourself" with a genius for experimentation, theatricality, and provocation. Writer Laura Barcella argues that Madonna "changed everything: the musical landscape, the '80s look *du jour*, and most significantly, what a mainstream female pop star could (and couldn't) say, do, or accomplish in the public eye." *Time Magazine* placed her on its 2010 list of the "25 Most Powerful Women of the Past Century." According to the *Guinness World Records*, she is the bestselling female artist of all time.

Madonna is such a commanding presence that it's hard to picture her ever feeling shy or insecure. But in an interview with *Vanity Fair*, she described her young self as "a lonely girl who was searching for something. ... I didn't shave my underarms and I didn't wear makeup like normal girls do. But I studied and I got good grades. ... I wanted to be somebody." Mission accomplished!

TALKING HEADS

The Talking Heads had released three studio albums and earned critical acclaim in the late 70s, but they really hit their stride in the 80s. Their 1983 single "Burning Down the House" reached number nine on the *Billboard* Hot 100 chart and number six on the *Billboard* Mainstream Rock Tracks chart. Their 1984 concert film *Stop Making Sense* (directed by future Academy Award-winning director Jonathan Demme) got rave reviews from major critics like Pauline Kael, Gene Siskel, and Roger Ebert. Their masterful album *Remain in Light* (1980)—which blended rock, funk, African music, and electronica—reached number 19 on the *Billboard* 200 and is widely regarded as one of the best albums of the 80s. Records like these would inspire many rock and pop acts, including Primus, Vampire Weekend, The 1975, and Kesha.

One of the Talking Heads' side projects made an impact as well. Bassist Tina Weymouth and drummer Chris Frantz formed the new wave band Tom Tom Club in 1981. Their dance hit "Genius of Love" was sampled by Grandmaster Flash and the Furious Five, L'Trimm, Redman and other hip-hop acts.

NEW ORDER

After singer Ian Curtis committed suicide in 1980, the three remaining members of Joy Division reformed as New Order. They soon began incorporating electronica and disco into their music and achieved far greater commercial success than the earlier band did. Their 1983 track "Blue Monday" became the best-selling 12" single of all time. Their blend of rock and dance music influenced groups like the Pet Shop Boys and the Killers.

In the early 2000s, New Order's lineup had a surprising addition: Smashing Pumpkins leader Billy Corgan. Corgan had a cameo on the band's album *Get Ready* (2001) and toured briefly with them in the UK, the US, and Japan.

BAUHAUS

It didn't take long for the British post-punk group Bauhaus to make their mark on rock history. They had only been a band for six weeks before they recorded their 1979 debut single, the eerie, nine-minute-long "Bela Lugosi's Dead." With its release, gothic rock was officially born.

Albums like *In the Flat Field* (1980) and *Mask* (1981) went further in defining the goth rock sound, combining dance rhythms with Daniel Ash's abrasive guitar lines and Peter Murphy's archly menacing vocals. Bauhaus broke up in 1983 but ended up influencing a wide variety of artists, including Danzig, Type O Negative, Marilyn Manson, Nine Inch Nails, Soundgarden, Interpol, My Chemical Romance, and the Dresden Dolls.

In spite of their wide-ranging influence, Bauhaus had only modest commercial success in the 80s. Their biggest hit was a cover of David Bowie's "Ziggy Stardust," which reached number 15 on the UK music charts. The band has another connection with Bowie: They appear briefly in the 1983 vampire film *The Hunger*, which starred Bowie and was directed by Tony Scott (*Top Gun*).

JUDAS PRIEST

Ever seen a metal band wearing biker or S&M gear? You can probably thank Judas Priest for that. The English band— particularly lead singer Rob Halford—helped popularize the leather-spikes-and-studs look that's a cliché in metal circles today.

Judas Priest's music has been plenty influential too. While late-70s albums like *Sin After Sin* (1977) and *Stained Class* (1978) helped set precedence for progressive metal bands like Tool and Dream Theater, their platinum albums *British Steel* (1980) and *Screaming for Vengeance* (1982) helped solidify mainstream culture's conception of heavy metal as a whole.

Given their super-tough look and sound, Judas Priest's origins may surprise you. The band started out playing blues in the late 60s. They took their name from Bob Dylan's cryptic folk song "The Ballad of Frankie Lee and Judas Priest." Also, none of the band members that most people know today such as Halford and guitarists K.K. Downing and Glenn Tipton were part of the original lineup. Downing and bassist Ian Hill joined the band in 1970. They recruited Halford around 1973 and other members after that.

MOTORHEAD

When Ian "Lemmy" Kilmister formed Motorhead in 1975, he had a clear idea of what he wanted the band to sound like. In his words, they'd make "loud, fast, city, raucous, arrogant, paranoid, speedfreak rock n' roll … It will be so loud that if we move in next door to you, your lawn will die."

The impact of Motorhead's music on their neighbor's lawns may be unknown, but it certainly lived up to the rest of Kilmister's vision. For 40 years, the British rock band combined the massive riffs of heavy metal with the breakneck speed of punk rock. They scored their biggest hits in the 80s with the classic albums *Ace of Spades* (1980) and *No Sleep 'til Hammersmith* (1981). Releases like these helped pave the way for speed metal and thrash metal.

Kilmister's life could be just as wild as his music. He started smoking at age 11 and claimed to have drunk a bottle of Jack Daniel's every day for almost 30 years. He is also believed to have slept with more than 1,000 women. "Sex, drugs and rock and roll" indeed!

BLACK FLAG

While the raw power of UK punk gave way to the moodiness and angularity of post-punk in the 80s, an even more violent form of punk emerged from the US West Coast. At ground zero of the blast was Black Flag, now largely recognized as the preeminent American hardcore group.

In addition to launching the career of singer-writer-actor Henry Rollins, Black Flag's abrasive guitar, disorienting tempo shifts, and experiments with jazz and metal inspired a variety of bands, including Nirvana, Slayer, and the Red Hot Chili Peppers. Not only that, guitarist-bandleader Greg Ginn founded SST Records, which put out recordings by major rock groups like the Minutemen, Bad Brains, Hüsker Dü, Sonic Youth, and Soundgarden.

While his band became infamous for their relentlessly aggressive music, Greg Ginn picked a surprisingly mellow band as his favorite: The Grateful Dead. "I saw them maybe seventy-five times," he told music writer Michael Azerrad. He also liked jazz, blues, country, and disco. Go figure!

Tom Waits

Tom Waits had earned a following in the 70s for music that drew heavily from jazz, Tin Pan Alley, and beatnik poetry. The music Waits started making in the 80s, however, was something completely different. On acclaimed albums like *Swordfishtrombones* (1983) and *Rain Dogs* (1985), he smashed together rock, cabaret, blues, spoken word, and whatever else seemed to pop into his head. His surreal lyrics and wildly eccentric tunes and instrumentation cemented his reputation as, in critic Robert Christgau's words, "the poet of America's non-nine-to-fivers."

A wide range of artists have covered Waits' songs over the years, including the Eagles and the Ramones. The songwriter hasn't always found imitation very flattering, though. In 1988, Waits sued the chip and snack manufacturer Frito-Lay for ripping of his song "Step Right Up" in a commercial. The 9th Circuit Court of Appeals ruled in Waits' favor and awarded him $2.375 million.

Van Halen

Highlighted by guitarist Eddie Van Halen's astonishing chops and lead singer David Lee Roth's wild-man persona, Van Halen put out two commercially successful albums in the late 70s. They didn't truly achieve superstar status, however, until the release of

1984 (1984). Their synthesizer-heavy single "Jump" earned a Grammy nomination and became their only number one hit. The album itself was held back from *Billboard*'s number one spot only by Michael Jackson's *Thriller*.

Fans see Roth as such a fundamental part of Van Halen that they may be surprised to learn that he didn't get in the band because of his singing. According to Eddie Van Halen, the band had been renting Roth's PA system in their early days. They hired him because they figured they could get the system for cheaper that way.

SONIC YOUTH

Until they broke up in 2011, no alternative rock band was more revered than Sonic Youth. Emerging from New York's short-lived no wave scene, the band built up considerable connections in the independent rock scene. They released highly praised albums like *Sister* (1987) and *Daydream Nation* (1988), whose mix of anthemic songs, idiosyncratic guitar tunings, and white noise experiments helped get them a deal with Geffen Records. And not only did they manage to retain control of their music, they also persuaded the label to sign a grungy rock trio from Seattle called Nirvana.

Not all critics warmed immediately to Sonic Youth. *Village Voice* music editor Robert Christgau, for instance, dismissed their self-titled debut EP (1982) and their first full-length album *Confusion is Sex* (1983) as boring, pretentious trash. Guitarist Thurston Moore grew so angry at Christgau—and at the *Voice* for what he considered their lack of support for New York bands—that he changed the name of the song "Kill Yr. Idols" to "I Killed Christgau with My Big Fucking Dick."

The vitriol mellowed out over time, though; in a 2006 article, Christgau went so far as to declare, "Sonic Youth are the best band in the universe, and if you can't get behind that, that's your problem."

THE SMITHS

Lead singer Morrissey once told an interviewer that he named his 80s band the Smiths because "it was the most ordinary name, and I thought it was time that the ordinary folk of the world showed their faces."

People might call the Smiths a lot of things, but ordinary probably won't be one of them. The Manchester band lasted from 1982 to 1987 and released four studio albums. Their swooning vocals, literate lyrics, and jangly guitar only gained a cult following in the US, but they inspired an almost religious fervor in the UK. BBC News once declared that the Smiths "inspired deeper devotion than any British group since the Beatles." They were a major influence on British groups like the Stone Roses, Oasis, and Blur.

In his Smiths days, Morrissey adopted a subdued, bookish appearance that contrasted sharply with the flashiness of New Romantic pop bands like A Flock of Seagulls and Duran Duran. Not that he didn't appreciate flashiness—as a boy, he adored glam rock acts like T. Rex and David Bowie. He even organized a UK fan club for the New York Dolls and wrote a 24-page booklet on them for Babylon Books. The latter achievement caught the attention of guitarist Johnny Marr, with whom Morrissey would start the Smiths.

U2

Originally called "Feedback" and "The Hype," the Irish rock band U2 formed in 1976 and became one of the biggest bands not just of the 80s but of all time. Their album *The Joshua Tree* (1987) was an international chart-topper and has become one of the all-time bestselling albums. Their unabashed romanticism and grandiosity have earned their share of taunts and criticisms over the years, but the band can cry about it on the way to the stadium—their tours still regularly gross more than $100 million.

U2 has always been politically outspoken (particularly their lead singer Bono). They've had to endure much more than harsh words because of this. While on tour for *The Joshua Tree*, Bono spoke out against the November 1987 bombing in Enniskillen, Ireland, which killed 11 people and wounded 63 more. As a result, the band received kidnapping threats and had their vehicle attacked by IRA supporters. In spite of these incidents, footage of Bono denouncing the bombing still made it into their 1988 concert film *Rattle and Hum*.

Say this much for U2: They don't back down!

STEVIE RAY VAUGHAN

Although he died in a helicopter accident at age 35, Stevie Ray Vaughan had done enough by that point to earn a spot in guitar god Valhalla next to Jimi Hendrix himself. Starting with their debut album *Texas Flood* in 1983, Vaughan and his band Double Trouble managed to bring pop culture attention back to the blues. Vaughan's fiery, staggeringly fluid guitar style earned him numerous accolades. *Rolling Stone* named him as the twelfth greatest guitarist of all time in 2011.

Before he released *Texas Flood*, mainstream audiences got a taste of what Vaughan could do on guitar with David Bowie's hit album *Let's Dance* (1983). Bowie invited him to play on the album after seeing him perform at the 1982 Montreux Jazz Festival. You can hear Vaughan soloing on the title track and the single "China Girl."

RUN-DMC

When we think of hip-hop today, a lot of what comes to mind stems from the influence of Run-DMC. Their "street" style—Kangol hats, gold chains, Adidas shoes—became the dominant look for rappers and their fans. They had the first rap album to go gold (1984's *Run-DMC*), the first one to go platinum (1985's *King of Rock*), and the first one to go multiplatinum (1986's *Raising Hell*). They combined rap and rock on hit singles like "Rock Box" and "Walk This Way" (which, incidentally, revived Aerosmith's career), bringing hip-hop further into the mainstream and inspiring rock groups like Faith No More, Red Hot Chili Peppers, and Rage Against the Machine to incorporate rap into their music. Their spare, tough music also defined what became known as "hardcore" hip-hop.

Considering how iconic the name "Run-DMC" has become, it's ironic that the group hated it at first. Producer and Def Jam Recordings cofounder Russell Simmons (the brother of "Run" aka Joseph Simmons) began marketing them with that name. At the time, DMC once told an interviewer, they all thought, "We're gonna be ruined!" Yeah, not so much…

THE POLICE

The Police got their start in the London punk scene in the 1970s, but they never fit in. As music critic Christopher Gable wrote, the trio "merely utilized the trappings of 1970s British punk… In fact, they were criticized by other punk bands for not being authentic and lacking 'street cred.'"

They might not have had street cred, but that didn't bother the pop market at large. In their ten-year run, the Police scored five number one UK albums in a row, starting with *Regatta de Blanc* (1979) and ending with *Synchronicity* (1983). The latter album featured the smash hit "Every Breath You Take," which beat out Michael Jackson's "Billie Jean" for the Song of the Year Grammy. According to music publisher Tom Bradley, money from that one song constituted ¼- ⅓ of ex-Police bassist Sting's entire music publishing income.

Recording "Every Breath You Take" wasn't easy. Sting and drummer Stuart Copeland fought constantly. Also, Copeland recorded his drum part in a room in the studio's dining room, which became so hot that he needed to have his drumsticks taped to his hands. Still, their work definitely paid off—in the early 2000s, Sting was still getting approximately $2,000 in royalties each day for that song.

REM

Characterized by Peter Buck's ringing guitar lines, Mike Mills and Bill Berry's driving rhythms, and Michael Stipe's slightly whiny but still pleasant vocals, REM's music served as the bridge between post-punk and alternative rock. The group formed in 1980 and earned considerable critical praise before breaking through commercially with their album *Document* (1987).

REM signed to Warner Bros. after the release of *Document*, a move that provided a template for other underground rock acts to follow. As Dream Syndicate bandleader Steve Wynn put it, "They invented a whole new ballgame for all of the other bands to follow, whether it was Sonic Youth or the Replacements of Nirvana or Butthole Surfers."

The group had never planned to hit it as big as they did. You can tell from the potential band names they kicked around, which included "Cans of Piss" and "Negro Wives." In the end, Stipe picked REM (an abbreviation of "rapid eye movement") from a dictionary. Sometimes, the spontaneous choice is the right one.

GUNS N' ROSES

In the late 80s, people started calling Guns N' Roses "the most dangerous band in the world." It was a well-earned title.

They fought with other bands, music critics, and each other. They lived the "Sex, Drugs, and Rock & Roll" lifestyle like few others did or could. Riots broke out at their concerts. They sparked intense controversy over their use of racist and homophobic slurs in the 1988 song "One in a Million" and their cover of a Charles Manson song on the album *The Spaghetti Incident* (1993). But in the midst of all this chaos, they produced galvanizing rock songs like "Welcome to the Jungle" and "Sweet Child o' Mine."

The best-known Guns N' Roses lineup is the one that played on their debut album *Appetite for Destruction* (1987): Lead singer Axl Rose, guitarists Slash and Izzy Stradlin, bassist Duff McKagan, and drummer Steven Adler. A bewildering number of musicians have worked with the band over the years, however, including Replacements bassist Tommy Stinson, Black Label Society leader Zakk Wylde, Nine Inch Nails drummer Chris Vrenna, and Queen guitarist Brian May.

RANDOM FUN FACTS

1. Back in 1988, Bruce Springsteen played a show near Washington, DC. In the crowd was Fawn Hall, secretary to Marine Corps Lt. Colonel Oliver North (she had helped him shred documents connected to the Iran-Contra scandal). Hall sent him a note backstage requesting to meet him. Springsteen sent back this reply: "I don't like you. I don't like your boss. I don't like what you did. Thank you."

2. The video for Madonna's hit song "Express Yourself" was directed by David Fincher, now best known for such acclaimed films as *Seven, Zodiac, The Curious Case of Benjamin Button,* and *The Social Network*.

3. "Weird Al" Yankovic has parodied numerous hit songs over the years. One of the only artists to turn down a parody was Prince, whose management company once sent Yankovic a telegram instructing him not to make eye contact with the "Purple One" at the American Music Awards (he wasn't being singled out, though; apparently, other people who sat near Prince at the awards show got the same telegram).

4. The British rock band Radiohead took their name from the song "Radio Head" off the Talking Heads' album *True Stories* (1986).

5. If you look closely at the 1984 music video for Chicago's soft-rock ballad "You're the Inspiration," you'll see that lead singer Peter Cetera is wearing a Bauhaus t-shirt. New Kids on the Block member Jordan Knight is wearing one too, in the 1988 video for the group's song "Please Don't Go Girl." Were Cetera and Knight secret Goths? Maybe they just liked vampires.

6. Motorhead's classic 1980 single "Ace of Spades" features a lot of poker references, but Lemmy Kilmister didn't care much for cards. "I'm more into slot machines actually," he wrote in his autobiography *White Line Fever*, "but you can't really sing about spinning fruit and the wheels coming down."

7. The music video for Michael Jackson's hit single "Bad" boasts quite a pedigree. It was written by novelist Richard Price (*Clockers*) and directed by Martin Scorsese (*Taxi Driver, Raging Bull*).

8. "I know someday that she'll wear my ring," Tom Waits sings on the 1980 ballad "Jersey Girl." He wasn't kidding: The song was inspired by artist Kathleen Brennan, who married Waits in August 1980. Waits credits Brennan with encouraging him to experiment more with his music. She's also listed as co-writer on many of his more recent songs.

9. After David Lee Roth left Van Halen, the group recruited Sammy Hagar as lead vocalist. Before they did, however, they asked two unlikely artists to take Roth's place: Scandal

vocalist Patty Smyth (best known for the hit songs "Goodbye to You" and "The Warrior") and Daryl Hall from Hall & Oates.

10. Sonic Youth's first drummer was Richard Edson, who is best known as an actor. He has had roles in a variety of acclaimed films, including *Stranger Than Paradise*, *Platoon*, *Good Morning Vietnam,* and *Do the Right Thing*.

11. Morrissey has an extremely devoted fan base among Mexican Americans. This following has been the subject of numerous news stories over the years. It has even inspired a Mexican tribute band called Mexrrissey.

12. When U2's Bono makes a public appearance, you'll almost always see him wearing shades. It's not that he's full of himself—he suffers from glaucoma and extreme sensitivity to light.

13. When Judas Priest's album *British Steel* (1980) first came out, it sold for only £3.99 in the UK (roughly $2 US at the time). The band's label, Columbia Records, ran ads that called the record "British Steal."

14. Black Flag's logo of four black vertical bars is one of the most famous images in punk rock. It was designed by artist Raymond Pettibon, brother of bandleader Greg Ginn. Pettibon also designed many of the band's posters and album covers.

15. The name of Stevie Ray Vaughan's band Double Trouble

comes from the title of a 1958 song by Chicago bluesman Otis Rush.

TEST YOURSELF – QUESTIONS AND ANSWERS

1. Which famous filmmaker directed the video for Michael Jackson's song "Thriller?"

A) John Landis
B) Francis Ford Coppola
C) Steven Spielberg

2. Who was the original lead singer in Black Flag?

A) Henry Rollins
B) Darby Crash
C) Keith Morris

3. Which rock star drummer substituted for Guns N' Roses' Steven Adler at the 1989 American Music Awards show?

A) Charlie Watts from the Rolling Stones
B) Max Weinberg from the E Street Band
C) Don Henley from the Eagles

4. Bruce Springsteen's eerie 1982 song "State Trooper" was inspired by which punk group?

A) The Misfits
B) Suicide
C) The Damned

5. Stevie Ray Vaughan played guitar on which hit dance song?

A) Michael Jackson's "Beat It"
B) James Brown's "Living in America"
C) George Clinton's "Atomic Dog"

ANSWERS

1. A

2. C

3. C

4. B

5. B

CHAPTER FOUR

ARTISTS OF THE 90S

Rock continued to expand and mutate in the 1990s. Grunge, rap-rock, Britpop, riot grrl, industrial rock, post-hardcore—these were just a few of the genres and movements that rose to prominence over the course of the decade. Let's take a look at some of the most exciting groups of that exciting time.

NIRVANA

Before Nirvana, alternative and indie rock flew largely beneath the radar. Groups like Sonic Youth and REM may have landed deals with major labels, but glam metal (aka "hair metal") groups like Mötley Crüe and Poison dominated the radio, TV, and most any other mainstream outlet for rock music.

But when Nirvana released their second album, *Nevermind* (1991), everything changed. The record's lead single, "Smells Like Teen Spirit," played constantly on radio and MTV and became a hit in the US, the UK, and many other countries. Thanks to the runaway success of the song and *Nevermind*, music writers started dubbing Kurt Cobain the unofficial voice of the Generation X (he didn't much like the title). Nirvana's surprising mainstream breakthrough also kick-started the so-called grunge movement, bringing attention to groups like Pearl Jam, Soundgarden, and Alice in Chains.

No one, including Nirvana, expected "Smells Like Teen Spirit" to become such a seminal song. Cobain himself told *Rolling Stone* that it had "such a clichéd riff" (lots of people noted the similarity between said riff and that of "More Than a Feeling" by arena-rock group Boston). Also, the title of the song came from a joke. While Cobain and Bikini Kill front-woman Kathleen Hanna were hanging out in a motel room one night, Hanna wrote "Kurt Smells Like Teen Spirit" on the wall (Cobain's then-girlfriend, Tobi Vail, wore Teen Spirit deodorant). In the end, you could say the joke was on everybody!

SMASHING PUMPKINS

Smashing Pumpkins never got much respect from people in the 90s alternative rock scene. Hüsker Dü singer-guitarist Bob Mould once called them "the grunge Monkees." Producer Steve Albini likened them to corporate rock group REO Speedwagon in a vitriolic letter to the *Chicago Reader*—"stylistically appropriate for the current college party scene, but ultimately insignificant," he elaborated.

Plenty of people in the US and the world at large liked them just fine, though. By the time that the Pumpkins' original lineup had broken up in 2000, they had sold more than 20 million albums. Their international hit records *Siamese Dream* (1993) and *Mellon Collie and the Infinite Sadness* (1995) are widely considered two of the best rock albums of the 90s.

In their heyday, Smashing Pumpkins embraced a wider range of musical genres than any other major alt-rock group. They mixed together psychedelic rock, prog-rock, heavy metal, acoustic folk, dream-pop, and electronica. Although they were best known for their massive, distorted guitar sound, they scored their biggest hit with the electro-pop single "1979" from *Mellon Collie*.

Ironically, "1979" almost didn't make it onto the album. Bandleader Billy Corgan told the *Chicago Tribune* that played an incomplete version of the song to producer Flood, who immediately gave it the thumbs-down. Still, Corgan "had a gut feeling about this song from the very beginning." He completed the song in four hours and played it for Flood the next day. After just one listen, the producer said, "It's on the album." Here's to gut feelings!

RED HOT CHILI PEPPERS

In the 80s, the Red Hot Chili Peppers released four albums, scored a couple of hit singles, and worked with the likes of George Clinton, Maceo Parker, and Gang of Four guitarist Andy Gill. They didn't really make it big, however, until the release of *Blood Sugar Sex Magik* (1991), which blended hard rock, funk, and rap. Featuring such hits as "Give It Away" and "Under the Bridge," the record would reach number three on the *Billboard* 200 chart and establish them as one of America's leading rock groups.

People who caught the sexual overtones of "Give It Away"—and really, they're not that hard to spot—may be surprised by the song's surprisingly altruistic inspiration. In his memoir *Scar Tissue*, Kiedis remembered a time when his then-girlfriend Nina Hagen gave him one of her leather jackets. She told him that "if you have a full closet and someone sees something they like, if you give it to them, the world is a better place." Hard to argue with logic like that (especially when it produces great songs)!

HOLE

Most lovers of rock music would agree that Hole lead singer Courtney Love isn't the easiest person to like. To this day, there are still people who believe that she killed her husband, Nirvana frontman Kurt Cobain (people also used to say that he wrote all the songs on Hole's 1994 album *Live Through This* too). She probably didn't (and he definitely didn't), but from her rampant drug use to incidents like punching Bikini Kill's Kathleen Hanna at the 1995 Lollapalooza, she's certainly done enough to rub people the wrong way.

But regardless of whether or not you like Love as a person, she made some of the strongest and most provocative rock and roll of the 90s. Hole's songs explicitly dealt with the social struggles women faced in the 90s and are still dealing with today. By doing so, Love and her bandmates helped inspire a variety of recent female artists, including Lana Del Rey, White Lung's Mish Way, Sky Ferreira, and Tegan and Sara.

While Hole is commonly grouped with grunge bands like Nirvana and Pearl Jam, but their name comes from a much older source. Love has said in interviews that the name came from a line in *Medea* by ancient Greek playwright Euripides: "There is a hole that pierces right through me." It certainly has a better ring than Love's other option, Sweet Baby Crystal Powered by God.

NINE INCH NAILS

Industrial rock music had been simmering and bubbling in the more outré precincts of post-punk and indie rock since the late 1970s. With the release of Nine Inch Nails' second album, *The Downward Spiral* (1994), the genre boiled over, blew the lid off the pot, and scalded eardrums across the world.

The brainchild of musician Trent Reznor, NIN had experienced a fair amount of success with its debut album *Pretty Hate Machine* (1989), which featured the rage-filled anthem "Head Like a Hole." The group built an audience thanks to an aggressive live show. It all came to a head with *The Downward Spiral*, which debuted at number two on the *Billboard* 200 chart and went on to sell more than nine million copies. Singles like "March of the Pigs" and "Closer" combined abrasive textures with pop catchiness and helped bring industrial rock into the mainstream. Today, Reznor continues to release music with NIN and writes soundtracks for films like *The Girl with the Dragon Tattoo* and *The Social Network*, the latter of which earned Trent Reznor and his collaborator Atticus Ross an Oscar for Best Original Score.

Reznor found a suitably grim setting in which to record the dark, nihilistic songs that would make up *The Downward Spiral*. He rented the Los Angeles house where actress Sharon Tate and her friends had been murdered by murdered by the Manson Family in 1969. Living and working there proved an (understandably) unsettling experience, particularly when Tate's sister Patti confronted Reznor one day.

He told *Rolling Stone* in 1997, "When she was talking to me, I realized for the first time, 'What if it was my sister?'... I went home and cried that night. It made me see there's another side to things, you know?" No kidding!

PJ HARVEY

When Kurt Cobain's journals were published in 2008, they included a list of his all-time favorite albums. It included *Dry* (1992) by PJ Harvey.

Although she's only had modest commercial success compared to the likes of Nirvana, plenty of others have responded as passionately to Harvey's mix of blues, rock, folk, and electronica. *Rolling Stone* named her Songwriter of the Year and Best New Female Singer in 1992. Her album *To Bring You My Love* (1995) was named Album of the Year by *Rolling Stone*, *The Village Voice*, *USA Today,* and other publications. In 1999, *Spin* ranked it, Public Enemy's *Fear of a Black Planet* (1990) and Nirvana's *Nevermind* (1991) as the three best albums of the 90s.

Harvey's first gig as a solo artist wasn't very auspicious. She and her band played a skittle alley (essentially a European bowling alley) in 1991. In a 2004 interview, Harvey said they had managed to clear out the place after just one song. Well, you've gotta start somewhere…

LIZ PHAIR

Remember how Steve Albini dissed Smashing Pumpkins in a letter to the *Chicago Reader*? He had some choice words in there for singer-songwriter Liz Phair too: "Liz Phair is Rickie Lee Jones (more talked about than heard, a persona completely unrooted in substance, and a fucking chore to listen to)…"

Ouch. Not everybody shared Albini's opinion of Phair, though. Matador Records co-owner Gerard Cosloy, for instance, told *Soundcloud* that he thought her songs were "very honest, very direct, certainly very original." *Village Voice* critic Robert Christgau agreed, giving her debut album on Matador, *Exile in Guyville* (1993), an "A" rating and calling her "a rebel, and if all goes well, also a pathfinder." He and other voters in the *Voice*'s annual Pazz & Jop poll picked it as the best album of the year.

Phair's subsequent releases have met with more mixed responses, but *Guyville* is still considered one of the best albums in the 90s. The cassettes that Phair made herself in the early 90s under the name Girly-Sound have become collectors' items too. One of Phair's more recent albums, *Funstyle* (2010), came with a bonus disc of 10 Girly-Sound tracks.

SARAH MCLACHLAN

Sarah McLachlan's high school yearbook had a prediction about her future. It said that she was "destined to become a famous rock star."

That yearbook was right! The Canadian singer-songwriter became an international star in the 90s thanks to her albums *Fumbling Towards Ecstasy* (1993) and *Surfacing* (1997). The latter album earned her two Grammys and four Juno awards and has sold more than 16 million copies around the world.

McLachlan didn't stop at making beautiful music either. She also launched the highly successful Lilith Fair tour in 1997, which brought attention to a wide variety of female artists. More recently, she has founded a music school for at-risk kids and helped raise millions of dollars for the ASPCA with a series of TV ads featuring her music.

McLachlan's music even helped save a hip-hop legend's life. In 1997, Darryl McDaniels (aka "DMC" from Run-DMC) went through a period of extreme depression. He was actively contemplating suicide when he heard McLachlan's song "Angel" on the radio. "I turned it on and I heard Sarah McLachlan's record, and something that day said, 'Life is good. It's good to be alive,'" McDaniels once said in an interview. McLachlan would later collaborate with McDaniels on the song "Just Like Me" from his solo album *Checks Thugs and Rock N Roll* (2006).

MY BLOODY VALENTINE

My Bloody Valentine only released one full-length album in the 90s, but boy, did they make it count. On *Loveless* (1991), the Irish rock band blended together indie rock, dream-pop, electronica, and other genres to create what *Clash Music* would later call "the magnum opus of the shoegazing genre." Electronic music innovator Brian Eno, Robert Smith from the Cure, and Trey Anastasio from Phish have all expressed their admiration for the album. My Bloody Valentine's work also influenced albums by Smashing Pumpkins, Hole, U2, and shoegaze bands like Ride and Slowdive.

My Bloody Valentine started recording what would become *Loveless* in 1989. Their label, Creation Records, believed initially that the band would only take five days to get all of the tracks done. It didn't quite turn out that way: The album took two years to complete and cost a reported €250,000, which prompted Creation to drop the group from its artist roster.

After *Loveless* came out, My Bloody Valentine wouldn't release another album for 22 years. Maybe they wanted to give everyone's eardrums a rest: In 2000, *Mojo* ranked the band's tour for *Loveless* as one of the two loudest tours of all time.

RADIOHEAD

Out of the 90s rock groups that are still active today, Radiohead may well be the most revered. The English group's third album, *OK Computer* (1997), established them as one of the most innovative and challenging rock bands in the world. Renowned British music critic Nick Kent went so far as to declare that the album "will be seen as the key record of 1997, the one to take rock forward instead of artfully revamping images and song-structures from an earlier era." *OK Computer* also went platinum in several countries and won the Grammy for Best Alternative Music Album.

Such praise and success didn't come to Radiohead overnight. At first, their debut single "Creep" failed to make much of an impression in their homeland. BBC Radio 1 refused to play the song when it came out in 1992 because it was "too depressing." However, the song became an international hit, which led to a reissue in 1993. This time around, "Creep" hit number seven on the UK Singles chart. Sometimes, it just takes a while for people to catch on!

PAVEMENT

Pavement never sold a lot of records—certainly not as many as, say, Weezer, who offered a more polished and pop-friendly version of their slacker geekiness—but they are widely considered one of the best and most influential indie-rock bands of all time. Their albums *Slanted and Enchanted* (1992) and *Crooked Rain, Crooked Rain* (1994) regularly place high on lists of the best albums of 90s.

Given their slovenly, tunefully caterwauling music, it's not too surprising that Pavement was always a rather fractious affair. Original drummer Gary Young would do stuff like hand out cabbage and mashed potatoes to concert-goers and run around in the middle of songs. Their set at the 1995 Lollapalooza festival was so desultory that people threw mud and rocks at them. When the band broke up in 2000, lead singer Stephen Malkmus left it to guitarist Scott Kannberg to tell the other band members.

Drummer Steve West didn't even know Pavement was over until he read about it online.

FUGAZI

Ian MacKaye had already left his mark on rock and roll before starting Fugazi. His 80s group Minor Threat was one of the most influential hardcore punk bands along with Black Flag and Bad Brains. His songs had also inspired the "straight edge" movement (he's expressed some ambivalence about this over the years). As if this weren't enough, his DIY label Dischord helped solidify the Washington, DC punk scene and inspired other scenes across the US.

With Fugazi, MacKaye expanded on his 80s accomplishments. Building on his initial vision of a band that was "like the Stooges with reggae," he and his bandmates combined heavy riffs with funk and reggae rhythms, idiosyncratic chord and song structures, and squealing distortion. By doing so, they helped pave the way for post-hardcore.

In addition to their innovative music, they stayed committed to a DIY ethos; they kept ticket prices as low as possible and played places like abandoned supermarkets and art galleries, encouraging people to think beyond rock show conventions. They also actively dissuaded slam-dancing and violence at their shows. In author Michael Azerrad's words, "Fugazi staked out the indie scene as the moral high ground of the music industry."

Fugazi took their independence seriously. In 1993, Atlantic

Records president Ahmet Ertegun tried to sign the band to his label. He offered them their own subsidiary and more than $10 million. They passed.

ELLIOTT SMITH

In a 1998 interview on Dutch television, Elliot Smith said, "I'm the wrong kind of person to be really big and famous."

He had a point. Reserved and prone to depression, Smith wasn't one for schmoozing and networking. His introspective, melodious songs stood in stark contrast to the raw power of 90s grunge bands (the success of his 1994 solo debut *Roman Candle* prompted the breakup of his band Heatmiser). He abused numerous substances and frequently talked about killing himself. His behavior grew increasingly erratic as he grew more famous. He died in 2003 from two stab wounds to the chest (police haven't been able to determine conclusively whether Smith stabbed himself or someone else did).

Smith's life had a lot of turmoil, but his music endures. His songs continue to inspire artists such as Seth Avett from the Avett Brothers and Jessica Lea Mayfield, who released an album of Smith covers together in 2015. Rilo Kiley, Pearl Jam, Ben Folds, and others have written tributes to Smith as well.

Elliott Smith was not actually Elliott Smith. He was born Steven Paul Smith in 1969. There are different theories why he chose to call himself "Elliott." Smith himself said that he thought "Steve" made him sound like a "jock" while "Steven" was "too bookish."

One of his junior high friends believes Smith didn't want to be confused with Journey drummer Steve Smith. Whatever his reasons, the name has certainly stuck.

JEFF BUCKLEY

Like Jimi Hendrix or Nick Drake, people wonder what Jeff Buckley would have done had he lived longer. His accidental drowning in 1997 cut short an immensely promising musical career. His sole studio album *Grace* (1993)—which features a haunting, unforgettable version of Leonard Cohen's song "Hallelujah"—is now considered a masterpiece. David Bowie once picked it as his "desert island" album. Buckley's talents also earned the admiration of such heavy-hitters as Jimmy Page, Elvis Costello, and Lou Reed (who expressed an interest in collaborating with him).

Buckley's father was singer-songwriter Tim Buckley, who had died when Jeff was eight years old. The two had never really had a relationship—Jeff had only met Tim once—and Jeff was reluctant to make a connection between his music and his father's. Still, he agreed to perform at a tribute concert for Tim Buckley as a way of paying his respects. It was a wise move: The concert—Buckley's first time singing in public—was a success and launched his career.

GREEN DAY

Green Day has plenty of haters. That's been the case since they moved from indie label Lookout Records to Reprise in 1994, a move that lost them many of their original punk fans.

Nonetheless, the pop-punk trio's success—particularly with their breakthrough album *Dookie* (1994)—helped pave the way for revitalization of punk and ska in the years that followed. That's one reason why they topped *Consequence of Sound*'s list of the 100 Best Pop Punk Bands. As music writer Collin Brennan put it, "Without Green Day, this list would have no reason to exist."

A major inspiration for lead singer Billie Joe Armstrong's songwriting is an ex-girlfriend known only as Amanda. Armstrong dated her while the band was coming up in the Berkeley, CA, punk scene, and she broke up with him just before *Dookie* came out, which left Armstrong extremely depressed. But however much it hurt, Amanda provided the fuel for songs on numerous Green Day albums, including *Dookie*, *Insomniac* (1995), and *American Idiot* (2004).

RAGE AGAINST THE MACHINE

You just need to look at the front of Rage Against the Machine's 1992 self-titled debut album to know you're in for something intense. The cover features a picture of Buddhist monk Thich Quang Duc, who set himself on fire in 1963 to protest the South Vietnamese government's persecution of Buddhists.

Rage Against the Machine's fiery, explicitly political mix of rap and metal suited such a powerful image. The album sold more than four million copies worldwide and established them as a major rock group. Their follow-up albums, *Evil Empire* (1996) and *The Battle of Los Angeles* (1999), were successful as well. Rage Against the Machine's music has been featured in films and video games and influenced the nu metal bands of the late 90s.

Success didn't make the band soften their political convictions. When they played on *Saturday Night Live* in 1996, they tried to hang upside-down American flags on their amps to protest guest host Steve Forbes, who was a Republican candidate for President at the time. They filmed the music video for their 1999 song "Sleep Now in the Fire" outside the New York Stock Exchange and caused its doors to close.

OASIS

With the release of their first album, *Definitely Maybe* (1994), Oasis got as big as you could seem to get in England. It shot to number one on the albums chart and became the quickest-selling debut record of all time in the UK. Their follow-up, (*What's the Story) Morning Glory?* (1995) took them even higher—it became the best-selling UK album of the 90s. It also reached number four on the *Billboard* 200 chart and topped albums charts in several countries. These records established Oasis as one of the leading Britpop bands along with Pulp, Suede, and Blur.

At the heart of Oasis was the combative relationship between brothers Noel and Liam Gallagher. Surprisingly, neither brother was an original member! Originally called the Rain, the group formed in 1991. Liam Gallagher joined after original guitarist Paul Arthurs left and suggested changing the band's name to Oasis. Noel requested to join after that on the condition that he'd be the only songwriter and bandleader. Despite the fights that the Gallagher brothers got into over the years, it's safe to say that Noel's demand worked out well.

BECK

Chances are good that no one was more surprised than Beck when his 1994 song "Loser" became a smash hit. He'd had the idea for the song for a few years, but he wrote the song and recorded it with producer Karl Stephenson in only six and a half hours. Ironically, "Loser" made Beck a winner in a big way: It hit number one on *Billboard*'s Hot Modern Rock Tracks chart and number 10 on its Hot 100 chart. In short order, Beck signed to Geffen Records and launched a career that has mixed together rock, electronica, country, blues, hip-hop, and several other musical genres.

Although Beck has dabbled in many kinds of music over the year, his main focus in his early days was folk music. He'd play old songs on the bus and at coffee shops. Eventually, he started improvising lyrics on the spot to make people laugh, which led to him writing absurdist, free-associative songs not unlike "Loser." It's funny how joking around can pay off for you!

BIKINI KILL

Founded in the late 80s, Bikini Kill spearheaded what became known in the 90s as the riot grrl movement, which combined fiercely uncompromising punk rock with a DIY ethos and radical feminism. During their live shows, the band would encourage female concert-goers to come to the front of the stage so they could participate more. In addition to making music, members of the band helped publish a variety of zines that delved into topics like reproductive rights, the patriarchy, and abuse. As a result of these endeavors, some have argued that the band—and the riot grrl movement as a whole—played a key role in the emergence of third-wave feminism.

Even from a young age, Bikini Kill lead singer Kathleen Hanna was passionate about feminism. In an interview with *BUST* magazine, she recalled cutting pictures out of the feminist magazine *Ms.* as a girl. She also remembered going with her mom to the Solidarity Day march in Washington DC in 1981, which "was the first time I had ever been in a big crowd of women yelling, and it really made me want to do it forever." So far, so good!

SLEATER-KINNEY

Sleater-Kinney emerged from the ashes of the riot grrl movement to become one of the most acclaimed bands of the past 25 years. The group formed in 1994 as a side project of Heavens to Betsy front-woman Corin Tucker and Excuse 17 guitarist Carrie Brownstein. However, Tucker and Brownstein began throwing their energy into Sleater-Kinney as their other bands fell apart.

The group's intricate, visceral music carried on riot grrl's project of questioning and reshaping gender, consumer, v and class norms. In 2001, music critic Greil Marcus declared them America's best rock band in an article for *Time*. The group went on hiatus in 2006 and returned in 2015 with the album *No Cities to Love* (2015), which many reviewers called the group's best record to date.

People may know Carrie Brownstein best for her work she started during Sleater-Kinney's nine-year hiatus. Brownstein co-writes and stars with Fred Armisen in the Emmy-winning TC series *Portlandia*.

RANDOM FUN FACTS

1. Hole lead singer Courtney Love sang with alternative rock group Faith No More in the early 80s. She didn't last very long, though; a member of the band said later that they wanted a "male energy."

2. Sarah McLachlan's hit song "Angel" was inspired by Smashing Pumpkins keyboardist Jonathan Melvoin, who died of a heroin overdose in 1996.

3. According to producer Steve Albini, PJ Harvey only ate potatoes while recording *Rid of Me* (1993). Well, a girl needs her fiber…

4. In addition to her own songwriting, Liz Phair has also worked on scores for TV shows, including *In Plain Sight* and the CW's remake of *90210*.

5. One of the key elements of My Bloody Valentine's harsh but ethereal sound is the dreamy vocals of Bilinda Butcher. According to Butcher, that dreaminess literally came about by dreaming; she'd often fall asleep before recording her vocals and need to be woken up.

6. Lots of people know the grunge rock band Nirvana. However, most people probably don't know the band used that name well before the Seattle trio did. Irish musician

Patrick Campbell-Lyons and Greek composer Alex Spyropoulos formed a psychedelic group called Nirvana in England in 1965. They released five albums between 1967 and 1972. In 1992, the English Nirvana sued the American Nirvana over the use of the name. They settled out of court for a reported $100,000.

7. Elliott Smith was an avid Beatles fan. During his live shows, he would frequently cover songs by the band or their solo projects. The last song Smith ever played in concert was "Long, Long, Long" from *The Beatles* (1968) aka "The White Album."

8. The liner notes of *Rage Against the Machine* (1992) include thanks to Ian MacKaye and his brother Alec. Lead singer Zach de la Rocha was straight edge for a while (he did take up smoking at some point, though).

9. For a little while, Smashing Pumpkins considered having filmmaker Spike Jonze (best known for directing Beastie Boys videos and such films as *Being John Malkovich* and *Adaptation*) direct the music video for "1979." He was too busy at the time, though.

10. Nine Inch Nails' Trent Reznor was a bit of a drama geek in high school. He played Professor Harold Hill in *The Music Man* ("Ya got trouble! / Right here in River City!"). His classmates voted him Best in Drama. He certainly lived up to that title!

11. Oasis frequently cited the Beatles as their biggest influence.

With this in mind, it was strangely appropriate that when original drummer Tony McCarroll sued the group over royalties in 1999, he hired Jens Hills. Four years earlier, Hills had helped original Beatles drummer Pete Best get €2 million from the Fab Four.

12. The Red Hot Chili Peppers brought some heavy hitters along with them on their *Blood Sugar Sex Magik* tour. Their openers were Smashing Pumpkins, Nirvana, and Pearl Jam (whose lineup would eventually feature the Peppers' original drummer, Jack Irons).

13. Bikini Kill's name was inspired by the 1967 British film called *The Million Eyes of Sumuru*, about a femme fatale who plots to take over the world by replacing male leaders with members of her all-female army. After riot grrl musician Lois Maffeo used the name for a performance piece, drummer Tobi Vail adopted it as the name of her band.

14. Sleater-Kinney's name comes from Sleater Kinney Road in Lacey, WA. In their early days, the band's rehearsal space was located there.

15. When Prince played the Coachella Valley Music and Arts Festival, his set included a cover of Radiohead's song "Creep." A smartphone video of the performance made it online, but Prince had it taken down. When the Associated Press mentioned this incident to lead singer Thom Yorke, he said, "Well, tell him to unblock it. It's our… song."

TEST YOURSELF – QUESTIONS AND ANSWERS

1. Which female rocker played with Courtney Love in the band Sugar Baby Doll?

A) Kim Gordon from Sonic Youth
B) Patty Schemel from Hole
C) Jennifer Finch from L7

2. Which former Richard Hell guitarist plays on Matthew Sweet's hit song "Girlfriend"?

A) Ivan Julian
B) Robert Quine
C) Tom Verlaine

3. Before she became famous, PJ Harvey tried to sing backup for which cult indie rock group?

A) Tortoise
B) Glass Eye
C) Slint

4. Radiohead opened for which acclaimed alternative rock group in 1995?

A) REM
B) Sonic Youth
C) Pearl Jam

5. Pavement made a guest appearance on which Cartoon Network show?

A) Space Ghost Coast to Coast

B) *Aqua Teen Hunger Force*
C) *The Venture Bros.*

ANSWERS

1. C

2. B

3. C

4. A

5. A

CHAPTER FIVE

GREAT ALBUMS OF THE 60S AND 70S

We've gone through a lot of great rock and roll (and some other stuff too) over the past few chapters. By this point, you might be interested in listening to some of the artists we've looked at. With this in mind, let's take the next two chapters to check out some of the best albums released from the 1960s up to the 1990s.

We'll start with 60s and 70s. You'll see some familiar names, but you'll also see some new ones. There's much more fantastic rock than we can include here, but this'll give you a good start!

HIGHWAY 61 REVISITED BY BOB DYLAN

On the A side of *Bringing It All Back Home* (1965), Bob Dylan started dabbling with electric rock and roll. With his next album, *Highway 61 Revisited* (1965), he went all in and unleashed his most ambitious and freewheeling music up to that point (and possibly ever). The album kicks off with its lead single, "Like a Rolling Stone," which was revolutionary for its surreal lyrics, chaotic rock backing, and six-minute-plus length. The rest of the album follows suit, resulting in one of the most startling and influential albums of the 60s.

Originally, "Like a Rolling Stone" wasn't a song. It started out as 10-20 pages of verse that Dylan had written. Dylan has said that he didn't start thinking of it as a song until he was playing piano one day and tried singing the verses. When he'd finished writing the song, Dylan recognized it as his "breakthrough." It sure was!

RUBBER SOUL BY THE BEATLES

What do you do when you're already the biggest and best rock and roll band in the world? You get even better. That's what the Beatles did, anyway, with their album *Rubber Soul* (1965).

The record represented a huge leap forward for the Fab Four. It marked the first time that they conceived of an album as a cohesive whole, not just a batch of songs. They mixed together a wide variety of music, including pop, folk-rock, and soul. They incorporated instruments like the sitar on the song "Norwegian Wood," which would inspire many Western musicians to experiment with elements of non-Western styles. Last but not least, their lyrics became more sophisticated and nuanced than they had been in the past.

Perhaps Rolling Stones managed Andrew Loog Oldham summed up the influence of *Rubber Soul* best. In his words, it was "the album that changed the musical world we lived in then to the one we still live in today."

Critics have noted the prominent influence of Bob Dylan and the

Byrds on *Rubber Soul*. The influence wasn't just musical: *Pitchfork* writer Scott Plagenhoef notes that Dylan had introduced the Beatles to marijuana, which helps account for the album's "patient pace and languid tones."

PET SOUNDS BY THE BEACH BOYS

When Brian Wilson listened to the Beatles' *Rubber Soul*, he told himself that he needed to step up his game. As a result, he composed, arranged, and produced nearly all of *Pet Sounds* (1966), which many regard as the Beach Boys' masterpiece. Wilson came up with stunningly intricate harmony parts and incorporated instruments ranging from flutes and harpsichords to Theremin and Coca-Cola cans. He also mixed together pop, jazz, and other genres. Thanks to Wilson's groundbreaking work, *Pet Sounds* helped pave the way for psychedelic rock, prog-rock, and chamber pop. Some critics also consider it the first rock concept album.

Pet Sounds even got props from classical and avant-garde artists. Composer Philip Glass once praised the album for "its willingness to abandon formula in favor of structural innovation, the introduction of classical elements in the arrangements, [and] production concepts in terms of overall sound which were novel at the time."

The Psychedelic Sounds of the 13th Floor Elevators by the 13th Floor Elevators

Highlighted by lead singer Roky Erickson's demented vocals and the electric jug of Tommy Hall, the 13th Floor Elevators were one of the most far-out of the 60s psychedelic rock bands. They didn't hit it as big as some of their contemporaries due in part to the erratic behavior of Hall and Erickson (who was committed to a mental hospital in 1969 after being arrested for possession of a marijuana joint). Nonetheless, the Elevators' music would influence a number of bands, including Television, ZZ Top, REM, and Big Brother and the Holding Company. In fact, Janis Joplin once considered joining the Elevators and may have modeled her singing style partially after Erickson's.

The Austin group's debut album, *The Psychedelic Sounds of the 13th Floor Elevators* (1966), features their only hit single, "You're Gonna Miss Me." The song reached number 55 on the *Billboard* Hot 100 chart. According to bassist Benny Thurman, the band was high on LSD when they recorded "You're Gonna Miss Me." Does this count as method acting?

The Doors by the Doors

The Doors' self-titled 1967 debut album established them as one of the most skilled rock bands of the time. The album combined elements of pop, rock, jazz, blues, classical music, and even cabaret (it features a cover of Bertold Brecht and Kurt Weill's song "Alabama Song").

The Doors featured some of the group's most famous songs. These include "Break On Through"—which combined a bossa nova groove, a guitar riff inspired by blues guitarist Elmore James' song "Shake Your Moneymaker," and an R&B influenced organ solo—and their breakthrough single "Light My Fire," which has been covered by Jose Feliciano, Al Green, Shirley Bassey, and other artists.

THE VELVET UNDERGROUND AND NICO BY THE VELVET UNDERGROUND

The Velvet Underground's 1967 debut album was almost completely ignored by critics and radio stations at the time. Today, it's recognized as one of the most important records of the 60s. It influenced several genres of popular music, including punk, grunge, shoegaze, and goth-rock.

One of *The Velvet Underground and Nico*'s most important songs is the seven-minute "Heroin," which features a hypnotically shifting tempo and John Cale's droning, screeching electric viola. A broad range of artists have covered the song, including Mazzy Star, Roky Erickson from the 13th Floor Elevators, Echo & the Bunnymen, and Billy Idol (whose version was called "one of the worst covers ever recorded" by music writer Stephen Thomas Erlewine). Mick Jagger also said that "Heroin" inspired the song "Stray Cat Blues" on the Rolling

Stones' classic album *Beggars Banquet* (1968). American composer David Lang even wrote a voice-and-cello version of the song. Brian Eno wasn't kidding about the Velvet Underground's influence (see Chapter 1)!

MOBY GRAPE BY MOBY GRAPE

The 60s San Francisco group Moby Grape never got as big as they should have been. In part, theirs was a case of "too much, too soon"—their label, Columbia Records, decided to release five singles from their self-titled 1967 debut album on the same day. Instead of dazzling record-buyers, it created the impression that Moby Grape was all hype. Disputes with their management and the mental health issues of guitarist Alexander "Skip" Spence also helped the group fizzle out.

Nonetheless, *Moby Grape* is recognized today as one of the greatest rock albums of the 60s, containing elements of country-rock, garage-rock, psychedelic rock, and power pop. Artists ranging from Led Zeppelin's Robert Plant and Bruce Springsteen to Cat Power have covered songs from the album.

CHEAP THRILLS BY BIG BROTHER AND THE HOLDING COMPANY

The last Big Brother album to feature Janis Joplin on lead vocals, *Cheap Thrills* (1968) is commonly considered Joplin's finest hour as a singer (on record, anyway). It features two of Joplin's signature songs, "Piece of My Heart" and "Ball and Chain." The album reached number one on *Billboards* Top LPs chart and was number 338 on *Rolling Stone*'s 2003 list of the 500 greatest albums of all time.

The cover of *Cheap Thrills* has become as famous as its music. It was drawn by renowned cartoonist Robert Crumb, creator of Fritz the Cat and the *Keep On Truckin'* comic strip. Originally, Crumb had expected that his art would go on the back cover of the album. However, Joplin liked Crumb's work so much that she insisted that Columbia put it on the front.

ELECTRIC LADYLAND BY THE JIMI HENDRIX EXPERIENCE

Both Jimi Hendrix's debut *Are You Experienced?* (1967) and his follow-up album *Axis: Bold as Love* (1968) contain their share of groundbreaking rock and roll. However, his third album with the Experience, *Electric Ladyland* (1969), stands as his masterpiece. Its 16 tracks fuse together hard rock, R&B, English pop, blues, and funk and feature Hendrix's boldest sonic experiments.

Recording *Electric Ladyland* was a long, complicated process. At times, there were so many people in the studio that bassist Noel Redding later commented, "It was a party, not a session." Also, Hendrix demanded several takes of songs—he and drummer Mitch Mitchell reportedly recorded the song "Gypsy Eyes" more than 50 times. Hendrix played many of the bass parts on the album as well.

TROUT MASK REPLICA BY CAPTAIN BEEFHEART AND THE MAGIC BAND

Lots of people didn't know what to make of *Trout Mask Replica* (1969) when it first came out. The album didn't even chart in the US. *Village Voice* critic Robert Christgau gave it a "B+" rating and stated, "I find it impossible to give this record an A because it is just too weird. But I'd like to."

Over time, however, more and more listeners started to come around to this double album by avant-garde rockers Captain Beefheart and the Magic Band. *Trout Mask Replica* showcases Captain Beefheart's (real name: Don Van Vliet) three-octave vocals and mixes traces of blues music with disorienting polyrhythm and atonal noise. It influenced such artists as Tom Waits and PJ Harvey and was added to the Library of Congress's National Recording Registry in 2010.

The music on *Trout Mask Replica* might sound completely chaotic and improvised, but it was actually planned out very deliberately. Beefheart and his band lived together in a rented house and rehearsed the songs for eight months. Beefheart wrote out many of the songs on piano (which he'd never played before!) When he played something he liked, drummer John French would write it down and work with Beefheart to cobble together songs and arrangements. Once a song was completed, the musicians would play it the same way every single time. Whew—just thinking about this whole process can exhaust you!

There's a Riot Goin' On by Sly and the Family Stone

With *There's a Riot Goin' On* (1971), the ebullience and optimism of Sly and the Family Stone's 60s work gave way to despair, cynicism, and paranoia. Part of this shift was due to bandleader Sly Stone's extreme drug use and increasingly erratic behavior. He recorded most of the album himself in his Bel Air home or at the Record Plant recording studio.

While *Riot*'s murky grimness turned some reviewers off when it came out, its dark, hypnotic power pulled more and more people in. The album's funky grooves influenced the jazz fusion work of Miles Davis and Herbie Hancock, Marvin Gaye, James Brown, and numerous hip-hop artists.

As drugged-out and jaded as Sly Stone had become by this point, some of his old hopefulness still peeked out. When an interviewer asked him in 1997 why *Riot*'s title track had no running time, he replied, "I felt there should be no riots."

I'm Still in Love with You by Al Green

Al Green had a small hit with the 1968 song "Back Up Train," but he didn't hit his creative and commercial stride until he joined forces with producer Willie Mitchell in 1969. Mitchell helped Green develop his smooth, delicate yet funky style, which he deployed to great effect on hit songs like "Let's Stay Together" and "Take Me to the River." Green's work with Mitchell in 70s established him as one of the best and most influential soul singers of all time.

Green and Mitchell first perfected their formula on the album *I'm Still in Love with You* (1972), which features the hit title track as well as the popular songs "Look What You Done for Me" and "Love and Happiness." Appropriately enough for such a sexy track, "Love and Happiness" was reportedly written by guitarist Teenie Hodges while he was watching TV and making out with his girlfriend. It has been covered by many artists over the years, including Etta James, Toots and the Maytals, and Living Colour.

EXILE ON MAIN ST. BY THE ROLLING STONES

If the Rolling Stones had stopped making music at the end of the 60s, they'd still be one of the greatest rock bands of all time. "Satisfaction," "Paint It Black," "Jumpin' Jack Flash," "Gimme Shelter"—the list of classic songs they'd written would be enough for at least two groups.

However, the Stones didn't release their true masterpiece until 1972. Not everybody recognized it at the time, though. *Rolling Stone* writer (and future Patti Smith guitarist) Lenny Kaye, for example, felt that "you can leave the album and still feel vaguely unsatisfied." You can't fault him too much—after all, a double album with no real standout singles and a sound so murky that you could barely make out what anyone's singing? What kind of masterpiece is that? Nonetheless, *Exile*'s reputation rose over the years to the point where it's now considered the band's finest hour, an exhilarating run through rock, blues, country, soul, and gospel.

Much of *Exile* was recorded at a house that guitarist Keith Richards had rented in southern France (which accounts for the murky sound). He'd begun injecting heroin, which kept him from recording at consistent times. Different members of the band and other musicians needed to cobble together tracks separately. But somehow, it all worked!

PRETZEL LOGIC BY STEELY DAN

Combining acerbic, twisted lyrics with offhand musical sophistication, Steely Dan aren't quite like any other group of the 70s (or any time, for that matter). Co-founders Donald Fagen and Walter Becker managed to combine jazz-influenced chord sequences and harmonies with pop catchiness. Their Rock and Roll Hall of Fame bio notes that this combination "allowed Steely Dan to connect with rock fans, especially those who were college-aged and -educated."

Steely Dan's ability to combine rock, pop, and jazz reached its apex with their third album, *Pretzel Logic* (1974), which was named album of the year by *NME* and reached number two in the *Village Voice*'s annual Pazz and Jop poll (Joni Mitchell's album *Court and Spark* took the number one spot). It features the single "Rikki Don't Lose that Number," which manages to lay a pop tune on top of blues-based verses and a jazzy chorus. In a 2006 article, *Entertainment Weekly* reported that the "Rikki" in the song was actually poet Rikki Ducornet, who had attended Bard College with Donald Fagen in the mid-to-late 60s (Fagen wouldn't confirm the story).

BORN TO RUN BY BRUCE SPRINGSTEEN

Decades after *Born to Run* (1975) had come out, Bruce Springsteen called the album "the dividing line."

This was true in more ways than one. Springsteen's third album highlighted the themes of maturity, class struggle, and emotional bonds that mark his work to this day. It also established him as a major rock artist, especially after *Time* and *Newsweek* ran stories on him and put him on their covers two months after the album's release.

Recording *Born to Run*, to put it mildly, sucked. If it didn't sell well, there was a good chance that Columbia Records would've given Springsteen and his band the boot. That put a lot of pressure on the musicians to deliver a hit. It took them almost six months just to complete the title track, with Springsteen overdubbing layers of guitars, horns, strings, glockenspiel, and more. He and his collaborators spent another eight months of grueling 14-16 hour sessions getting the record done. When Springsteen finally heard the mastered version of *Born to Run*, he got so upset that he threw the record into a swimming pool and declared he'd trash the whole project. Thankfully, cooler heads prevailed, and the rest is history.

HORSES BY PATTI SMITH

Before *Horses* (1975) came out, Patti Smith was a poet, occasional journalist, and performance artist with one single to her name: "Hey Joe / Piss Factory." The release of her debut album, however, established her as one of the leading figures of a new rock genre called punk. British music critic Simon Reynolds once called it "the spark that ignited the punk explosion," noting that it came out five months before the Ramones' first album. Smith and her record would inspire female rockers like Courtney Love, as well as bands like the Smiths and REM.

Horses has a connection to the very wellspring of punk; it was produced by former Velvet Underground viola player John Cale (he also produced the 1969 self-titled debut album of Detroit proto-punks the Stooges). In proper punk fashion, Smith and Cale frequently butted heads during the recording of the album. Smith told *Rolling Stone*, "All I was really looking for was a technical person. Instead, I got a total maniac artist." For his part, Cale described working with Smith as "a lot like an immutable force meeting an immovable object." In spite of any friction that arose, Smith, her band, and Cale managed to make one of the best rock albums of all time.

The cover of *Horses*—which shows an androgynous-looking Smith wearing a white men's shirt—is as famous as its music. Though she'd later deny making any kind of statement with this image, it contrasted sharply with the soft, feminine look of most female artists up to that point. The photo was taken by artist Robert Mapplethorpe, whose pictures of black male nudes and New York's S&M subculture sparked intense controversy.

RUMOURS BY FLEETWOOD MAC

A lot of the albums described in this chapter were difficult to make, but *Rumours* (1977) stands in a category all by itself. Bassist John McVie and singer-keyboardist Christine McVie had recently divorced. Singer-guitarist Lindsey Buckingham and singer Stevie Nicks were also in an extremely combative relationship. Meanwhile, drummer Mick Fleetwood had learned that his wife had been sleeping with his best friend. Add to this all the cocaine that money could buy and all-night recording sessions (which, according to studio owner Chris Stone, wouldn't really start until the band got exhausted from partying), and you had a recipe for disaster.

But through a mix of talent, will, and pure luck, *Rumours* was anything but. It became Fleetwood Mac's second number one record in the US, sitting on top of the *Billboard* 200 chart for 31 weeks in all. To date, *Rumours* has sold more than 40 million copies around the world and influenced artists ranging from Tori Amos to Lorde.

Though Fleetwood Mac is best known for its 70s lineup of Buckingham, Nicks et al, Fleetwood Mac actually started as a British blues group in the late 60s. It featured guitarist Peter Green, who had played with John Mayall and the Bluesbreakers. They recorded a handful of hits, including "The Green Manalishi (With the Two-Prong Crown)," which heavy metal group Judas Priest covered on their album *Hell Bent for Leather* (1979).

NEVER MIND THE BOLLOCKS, HERE'S THE SEX PISTOLS BY THE SEX PISTOLS

By the time that the Sex Pistols released their debut album, they were already the most controversial rock group in the UK. After they'd cursed during an interview with Bill Grundy on Thames Television's *Today* program, the tabloids jumped all over it (one story in the *Daily Mirror* featured the now-famous headline, "The Filth and the Fury!"). Other incidents like vomiting in Heathrow Airport and wreaking havoc at the offices of A&M (which caused the label to drop the band from their contract after less than a week) further cemented their reputation as the ultimate bad boys.

Released by Virgin Records, *Never Mind the Bollocks, Here's the Sex Pistols* (1978) stirred up controversy with its very name. London police threatened Virgin record stores with charges of obscenity for displaying the word "bollocks" (i.e. testicles) in public. After one store manager was arrested, Virgin owner Richard Branson paid for his defense (he was later found not guilty of all charges). Ultimately, *Never Mind the Bollocks* made it out into the world and became one of the definitive punk albums.

PARALLEL LINES BY BLONDIE

Almost anyone who has listened to classic rock radio stations has most likely heard at least two songs from *Parallel Lines* (1978): the hard-rocking "One Way or Another" and the disco crossover smash "Heart of Glass," which hit number one in the US, the UK, and several other countries. But surprisingly, neither of these songs were the lead single off the album that finally made the New York band Blondie stars in their home country. Instead, Chrysalis Records picked the band's tossed-off cover of the Buddy Holly song "I'm Gonna Love You Too." Maybe they were shooting for the Belgium and Netherlands markets—those were the only places where the single charted!

That misstep aside, *Parallel Lines* was a huge success, selling 20 million copies as of 2010. Critics like Robert Christgau and Sasha Frere-Jones have called it a perfect pop-rock album. That perfection didn't come easily—producer Mike Chapman spent hours recording and rerecording guitarist Chris Stein's parts (it probably didn't help that Stein was high on drugs during the sessions). At various times during the recording process, Chapman recalled, lead singer Deborah Harry would slip into the restroom and stay there for hours. In spite of all the drama and painstaking care, Chapman and the band managed to finish recording the album in six weeks instead of the six months that Chrysalis gave them.

RUST NEVER SLEEPS BY NEIL YOUNG & CRAZY HORSE

Over the course of the 70s, you could've more or less split Neil Young's music into two halves. On the one hand, there was the folk and country of albums like *Harvest* (1972) and *Comes a Time* (1978), as well as his work with Crosby, Stills and Nash. On the other, there was the dark, intense rock and roll of records like *On the Beach* (1974), *Tonight's the Night* (1975), and *Zuma* (1976). With *Rust Never Sleeps* (1979), Young brought the two halves together—folk on side A, rock on side B—and created a summation of his work up to that point as well as an ode to personal and creative renewal.

Rolling Stone's critics voted *Rust Never Sleeps* Album of the Year. Fifteen years later, Nirvana's Kurt Cobain would pay a grislier tribute to Young's work—he quoted the line "It's better to burn out than to fade away" from the *Rust*'s lead track, "My My, Hey Hey (Out of the Blue)," in his suicide note.

The phrase "rust never sleeps" came from the post-punk band Devo. Young had heard members of the band chanting it. When he asked them what it meant, they replied that they'd come up with it for the Rust-Oleum brand of paints and coatings. Inspiration comes from all kinds of places!

RANDOM FUN FACTS

1. Some people speculate that the main character in Bob Dylan's song "Like a Rolling Stone" was inspired by Andy Warhol "superstar" Edie Sedgwick, who also provided the inspiration for the Velvet Underground song "Femme Fatale." Others believe that it's Dylan himself. Given the plethora of allusions and references throughout *Highway 61 Revisited*, who knows? It could be both. Or neither.

2. In concert, 70s rock band Television would frequently cover the song "Fire Engine" from *The Psychedelic Sounds of the 13th Floor Elevators*.

3. Denis Johnson's acclaimed book of short stories *Jesus' Son* takes its title from a lyric in the Velvet Underground's song "Heroin."

4. Before joining Moby Grape, guitarist Jerry Miller played with Texas rock and roller Bobby Fuller, who is best known for his 1965 hit "I Fought the Law." Miller actually played on a version of that song that Fuller had recorded earlier (but not on the one that became a hit).

5. While recording *Electric Ladyland*, Jimi Hendrix sat in on a spontaneous jam with influential bluesman B.B. King, keyboardist Al Kooper (who was a major contributor to

Highway 61 Revisited), and respected blues guitarist Elvin Bishop. You can find bootleg recordings of the show on Youtube (unless someone takes them down).

6. Recording *Trout Mask Replica* was difficult for Captain Beefheart and the Magic Band. The musicians were nearly broke most of the time and lived off welfare and gifts from family. French recalled eating only a cup of soybeans each day for a month. At one point, some of the musicians became so desperate for food that they resorted to shoplifting. When they got arrested, Zappa had to bail them out. Talk about suffering for your art!

7. *Rubber Soul*'s title came from a term that black musicians used to describe the Rolling Stones' lead singer Mick Jagger: "Plastic soul." It signified what they thought of a white Englishman singing black music. Well, when life hands you lemons...

8. The title of the Beach Boys' album *Pet Sounds* is partially a tribute to one of Brian Wilson's main inspirations, music producer Phil Spector. Note how the record and Spector have the same initials.

9. Sly and the Family Stone's album *There's a Riot Goin' On* features the number-one single "Family Affair," which is one of the first hit songs that uses a drum machine.

10. The Talking Heads scored their first top 30 hit with a cover of Al Green's "Take Me to the River," which appeared on their second album *More Songs About Buildings and Food*

(1978). In *Pitchfork* contributor Nick Sylvester's view, the single enabled the new wave group to break through to the mainstream.

11. The "exile" in *Exile on Main St.* comes from the fact that the Rolling Stones were dodging the taxmen in England. They'd fled to France to prevent them from seizing their assets.

12. Bruce Springsteen took the title for his song "Thunder Road" from a Robert Mitchum movie of the same name. According to Springsteen, he hadn't actually seen the movie—he just saw a poster for it.

13. *The Doors* features the haunting song "The Crystal Ship." According to legends spread around by Santa Barbara, CA, residents, lead singer Jim Morrison was inspired to write the song while tripping on LSD and staring at an oil rig off the Santa Barbara coast.

14. On the song "Land" from *Horses*, Patti Smith describes a character named Johnny. She drew inspiration for this figure from a character with the same name in William Burroughs' 1971 novel *The Wild Boys*. (Incidentally, David Bowie modeled the look of Ziggy Stardust and the Spiders from Mars after the titular characters.)

15. The band Steely Dan took its name from the William Burroughs novel *Naked Lunch*. In the book, "Steely Dan" is a dildo.

TEST YOURSELF – QUESTIONS AND ANSWERS

1. Which member of Moby Grape played with Jefferson Airplane and Quicksilver Messenger Service?

A) Skip Spence

B) Jerry Miller

C) Peter Lewis

2. Which record producer worked on Bob Dylan's *Highway 61 Revisited*, the Velvet Underground's *The Velvet Underground and Nico* and Simon and Garfunkel's single "The Sound of Silence"?

A) Tom Wilson

B) Bob Johnston

C) Tom Dowd

3. Who plays organ on the 15-minute blues jam version of "Voodoo Chile" on the Jimi Hendrix Experience's *Electric Ladyland*?

A) Ray Manzarek

B) Steve Winwood

C) Nicky Hopkins

4) Which blues-rock guitarist plays lead on Bob Dylan's album *Highway 61 Revisited*?

A) Robbie Robertson

B) Eric Clapton

C) Mike Bloomfield

5. Which experimental musician produced Captain Beefheart's album *Trout Mask Replica*?

A) Syd Barrett
B) John Cage
C) Frank Zappa

ANSWERS

1. A

2. A

3. B

4. C

5. C

CHAPTER SIX

GREAT ALBUMS OF THE 80S AND 90S

In this final chapter, we'll take a look at some of the best albums to come out in the 80s and 90s. There's everything from young punks flying right and breaking through to old-timers getting their grooves back. Enjoy! And keep rockin'!

LONDON CALLING BY THE CLASH

Depending on which side of the pond (i.e. the Atlantic Ocean) you're on, this could be one of the best albums of the 70s or the 80s. In the UK, *London Calling* came out in December 1979. In the US, it came out in January 1980.

Regardless of when it came out, *London Calling* immediately gained recognition as the Clash's best album to date. On its 19 tracks, the British band stretched well beyond punk's standard two-minute, three chord bursts; they incorporated reggae, funk, rockabilly, ska, and several other genres into their music. While the title song made it to number 11 on the UK singles chart, the infectious dance tune "Train in Vain" reached number 23 in the US. The album itself sold two million copies upon its release. It stands today as both the Clash's masterpiece and one of the greatest rock albums, period.

London Calling was produced by Guy Stevens, who had previously worked with rock band Mott the Hoople (a major influence on Clash guitarist Mick Jones). The Clash had tried recording with Stevens back in 1976, but the results were disappointing. Stevens had also managed to hit lead singer Joe Strummer in the eye with a record when they first met!

Stevens' approach to record production on *London Calling* was unorthodox, to say the least. While the Clash laid down tracks, he'd yell at them and smash furniture (Clash roadie Johnny Green remembered Stevens swinging an aluminum ladder at the band once). There was a method to his madness, though—his antics fired the Clash up and made them buckle down. Stevens may have been a nut, but he got results!

THE BLUE MASK BY LOU REED

By the time "Godfather of Punk" Lou Reed released *The Blue Mask* (1982), his wild days were mostly behind him. He'd spent a good chunk of the 70s binging on booze and drugs. For every success like the David Bowie-produced *Transformer* (1972) or the US top 10 album *Sally Can't Dance* (1974), there was a career-suicide move like *Metal Machine Music* (1975), a double album of pure feedback.

In the 80s, however, he started straightening up and flying right. He married artist Sylvia Morales in 1980 and quit drugs and drinking. Instead of living wild, Reed put the wildness into his music—on songs like *The Blue Mask*'s title track and "Waves of Fear," he and his band unleashed the same mix of pop songcraft and screeching distortion that Reed had pioneered in his Velvet Underground days. The album wasn't a hit, but longtime fans and critics hailed it as a bracing return to form. Rob Sheffield wrote in a 2012 appreciation of the record, "It's one of the toughest, truest, funniest albums about husbandhood ever made."

A big part of the credit for *The Blue Mask*'s power goes to guitarist Robert Quine. Reed had seen Quine play with Richard Hell and the Voidoids. When he invited Quine to join his band, Quine said he'd only accept if Reed started playing guitar again (Reed's atonal solos with the Velvet Underground were a big inspiration for Quine). The alternately searing and gorgeous interplay between Quine and Reed is one reason why *The Blue Mask* is possibly Reed's best solo album.

WILD GIFT BY X

Although they never truly achieved mainstream success, the Los Angeles punk band X attracted their fair share of devoted fans. One of them was Doors keyboardist Ray Manzarek, who produced X's first four albums. Others were Joan Jett, Black Flag lead singer Henry Rollins, Old 97s frontman Rhett Miller, and Pixies lead singer Frank Black (aka Black Francis). The 90s electronica star Moby once had this to say about the band: "For me, X represented what an unintentionally strange and fecund place America can be for the lovely and joyful perversions of the human spirit."

None of X's albums captured those "lovely and joyful perversions" better than *Wild Gift* (1981). The follow-up to their dark, full-throttle debut *Los Angeles* (1980), *Wild Gift* combined Captain Beefheart-inspired angularity, rockabilly guitar, and dissonant harmonies with vivid depictions of scenes from the L.A. punk subculture. It placed second in the *Village Voice*'s 1981 Pazz and Jop poll (the Clash's triple-album *Sandinista!* (1981) got first place).

Sadly, critical acclaim didn't translate into albums sold. X's closest brush with the mainstream might have been when their cover of the Troggs' garage rock classic "Wild Thing" appeared on the soundtrack for the 1989 film *Major League*.

PURPLE RAIN BY PRINCE

From 1980 to 1983, Prince had racked up a more than respectable number of hits with albums like *Controversy* (1981) and *1999* (1982). However, with the release of the film *Purple Rain* and its accompanying soundtrack in 1984, he went supernova. Starring Prince, Apollonia Kotero, and Morris Day, and loosely based on Prince's own life, the movie grossed more than $68 million in the US and won an Oscar for Best Original Song Score. The *Purple Rain* album stayed at the top of the *Billboard* 200 chart for 24 weeks in a row and sold over 25 million copies worldwide. The singles "When Doves Cry," "Let's Go Crazy," and "Purple Rain" were all big hits, with the first two songs reaching number one the *Billboard* Hot 100 and the third reaching number two.

Even *Purple Rain*'s deleted scenes would pay off dividends for the Purple One. A scene where Prince and Apollonia have sex in a barn was cut from the film, but Prince used it as the inspiration for the song "Raspberry Beret," which made it to number two on the Hot 100 in 1985.

LET IT BE BY THE REPLACEMENTS

American underground rock didn't want for anarchic live shows in the 1980s. Still, a Replacements concert back in the day was on a whole other level.

In his 2001 book *Our Band Could Be Your Life*, author Michael Azerrad recalls that the Replacements would "screw up a gig at the drop of a beer can; they'd toss their instruments around the stage, hand them to members of the audience to play, or stumble through an hour and a half of cheesy covers. Sometimes they demanded that unless the audience threw money onto the stage, they'd keep playing badly."

But by 1984, chaos like this was starting to get old. So, the band buckled down and came up with *Let It Be* (1984), which, in critic Robert Christgau's view, "stands beside *Wild Gift* as Amerindie's very peak." Smashing together hardcore, hard rock, country, and blues, the album boasted the band's most complex arrangements up to that point. Not only that, lead singer and songwriter Paul Westerberg's lyrics revealed a surprising pathos and thoughtfulness. Thanks to this newfound sophistication and focus, *Let It Be* would earn rave reviews from critics and influence bands ranging from the Goo Goo Dolls to the

Decemberists.

While the Replacements took *Let It Be* seriously, they didn't lose their sense of humor. The album's title was a joke both on the Beatles' 1970 album of the same name and their manager, Peter Jesperson (he was a big Beatles fan). Westerberg once said that the band had even considered naming their follow-up album *Let It Bleed* after the classic 1969 Rolling Stones record.

GRACELAND BY PAUL SIMON

Overall, the early-to-mid 80s were a rough time for singer-songwriter Paul Simon. His free 1981 concert in Central Park with his old musical partner Art Garfunkel had been a huge success; it attracted more than half a million people, making it the seventh largest live show in US history. Also, the album of the show went double platinum in America and charted high in several other countries. Unfortunately, Simon and Garfunkel couldn't get along long enough to make another album. To make matters worse, Simon split from his wife, actress Carrie Fisher, and received the worst sales of his career for the album *Hearts and Bones* (1983).

Then in 1984, Simon got his hands on a bootleg tape of South African music. What he heard inspired him so much that he went down to Johannesburg and recorded with local musicians for two weeks. Out of those recordings came *Graceland* (1986), which became Simon's best-selling solo album and won the 1987 Grammy for Album of the Year. It would go on to inspire artists like Bombay Bicycle Club, Regina Spektor, and Vampire

Weekend.

Not everyone was a fan of Simon's work on *Graceland*, though. By recording in Johannesburg, Simon broke the United Nations' cultural boycott on South Africa and its apartheid-supporting government. This aroused the ire of antiapartheid organizations and even the African National Congress, which voted to ban him from South Africa (the ban was later lifted). Still, the album helped the South African musicians who performed on it achieve worldwide popularity. These included the vocal group Ladysmith Black Mambazo, which has released several gold and platinum albums.

DAYDREAM NATION BY SONIC YOUTH

By the mid 80s, Sonic Youth was getting more and more recognition. Critic Robert Palmer wrote in the *New York Times* that they were "making the most startlingly original guitar-based music since Jimi Hendrix." With the release of their double album *Daydream Nation* (1988), the praise reached critical mass. The *NME* called it the "most radical and political album of the year." The *Record Mirror* went even further and declared that Sonic Youth was "the best band in the universe."

Sonic Youth drew inspiration from a wide variety of sources for *Daydream Nation*'s songs. "The Sprawl" took its name from a massive, futuristic city in sci-fi writer William Gibson's stories and borrowed lines from Denis Johnson's novel *The Stars at Noon*. "Hey Joni" is a tribute to Joni Mitchell, whom guitarists Lee Ranaldo and Thurston Moore both cited as an influence.

Also, the band had originally considered calling the album *Tonight's the Day* partially as a nod to Neil Young's album *Tonight's the Night* (1975).

IT TAKES A NATION OF MILLIONS TO HOLD US BACK BY PUBLIC ENEMY

Public Enemy's debut album, *Yo! Bum Rush the Show* (1987), didn't get a lot of mainstream attention. The hip-hop group's follow-up, *It Takes a Nation of Millions to Hold Us Back* (1988), proved impossible to ignore. Originally called *Countdown to Armageddon*, *Nation of Millions* combined confrontational, politically charged lyrics with, in critic Robert Christgau's words, "post-Coleman/Coltrane ear-wrench." The double album's dense, abrasive collages of samples—which came courtesy of the hip-hop production team known as the Bomb Squad—was virtually unprecedented in hip-hop or any other genre of popular music.

Nation of Millions went platinum in the US and topped the 1988 *Village Voice* Pazz and Jop poll. Today, it is considered one of the best albums of all time in any genre (Kurt Cobain from Nirvana included it in a list of his 25 favorite albums).

Public Enemy and the Bomb Squad sampled a huge number of records to make the album (one track, "Night of the Living Baseheads," pulls from a whopping 21 songs). Perhaps it's only fair that numerous artists have taken samples from *Nation of Millions* over the years. These include the Beastie Boys,

Madonna, My Bloody Valentine, and Jay-Z.

SURFER ROSA BY THE PIXIES

When Nirvana had finished "Smells Like Teen Spirit," both Kurt Cobain and bassist Krist Novoselic reportedly worried that it sounded too much like the Pixies. At least they were upfront about the similarities: Cobain would later cite the alternative rock band's debut album *Surfer Rosa* (1988) as the primary inspiration for the songwriting on *Nevermind* (1991).

Nirvana wasn't the only group inspired by *Surfer Rosa*. Although it didn't sell very well upon its release, the record has become one of the most influential rock albums of the 1980s. Billy Corgan from the Smashing Pumpkins, for instance, recalled being blown away when he first heard the album: "It was so fresh. It rocked without being lame." PJ Harvey was equally impressed—she got *Surfer Rosa*'s producer, Steve Albini, to produce her dark, raw sophomore album *Rid of Me* (1993).

Even David Bowie dug the Pixies' catchy, cryptic songwriting. He covered the song "Cactus" from *Surfer Rosa* on his album *Heathen* (2002).

COSMIC THING BY THE B-52S

In a way, it's amazing that the B-52s managed to put out *Cosmic Thing* (1989) at all. The new wave band had been reeling from the loss of guitarist Ricky Wilson, who had died of AIDS in 1985. Drummer Keith Strickland had managed to figure out how to play guitar like Wilson, which allowed them to complete the album *Bouncing Off the Satellites* (1986). However, the band was too depressed to tour behind the album and went on hiatus for the next two years.

Then in 1988, Strickland played some new music he'd been working on to the remaining band members. Singers Fred Schneider, Kate Pierson, and Cindy Wilson liked what they heard enough to figure out some tunes and lyrics to go with it. The end result was *Cosmic Thing* (1989), the B-52s' biggest commercial success. It produced the hit singles "Channel Z" and "Roam."

However, the biggest hit off *Cosmic Thing*—and the group's best-selling single of all time—was the irresistible "Love Shack." The song was inspired by a cabin near Athens, Georgia, where Kate Pierson lived back in the 70s (the B-52s wrote one of their most famous songs, "Rock Lobster," there). If you've heard it—and really, who hasn't?—you'll know the part where Cindy Wilson shouts, "Tin roof! Rusted." That was actually an outtake that they stuck on the track later. (By the way, Pierson's cabin actually had a tin roof.)

NEVERMIND BY NIRVANA

Kurt Cobain once said that he wanted *Nevermind* (1991) to sound like "the Knack and the Bay City Rollers getting molested by Black Flag and Black Sabbath." Combining catchy melodies with roaring distortion, angst-filled lyrics, and muscular beats, Nirvana achieved that goal. In the process, they changed the course of rock and roll in the 90s by ushering in the grunge movement.

Geffen Records didn't expect *Nevermind* to be a blockbuster—they figured it might go gold (i.e. sell half a million copies) by September 1992 with some heavy promotion. But thanks in no small part to the runaway popularity of "Smells Like Teen Spirit," *Nevermind* reached the top of *Billboard*'s album chart on January 11, 1992. As Geffen president said to *The New York Times*, "We didn't do anything. It was just one of those 'Get out of the way and duck' records."

According to bassist Krist Novoselic, the album's title came from the cynicism that he and his bandmates felt over public response to the 1990-91 Gulf War. Originally, Cobain had wanted to call the album *Sheep* as a joke on the people he figured would buy the record. Well, at least you couldn't accuse Cobain of pandering...

BRICKS ARE HEAVY BY L7

Butch Vig was a busy boy in the early 90s. In addition to *Nevermind* and Sonic Youth's raucous album *Dirty* (1992), he produced this album by all-female Los Angeles hard rock band L7. While it wasn't a smash hit like Nirvana's album, *Bricks Are Heavy* (1992) did make it to number one on the *Billboard* Top Heatseekers chart and sold reasonably well in the UK and Australia. The album's anti-Moral Majority single "Pretend We're Dead" was a hit on the Alternative Songs chart and MTV.

"Pretend We're Dead" also scored L7 appearances on the UK TV shows *Top of the Pops* and *The Word*. On the latter show, singer-guitarist Donita Sparks pulled down her jeans in the middle of the song, revealing to late-night audiences that she wasn't wearing any underwear.

"There was also a bare bum contest going on [as part of the show]," Sparks told *Dazed* in 2016. "I suppose it was fun, but I was also like, 'Fuck it, this is live TV, I'm dropping my pants. Why not, anything goes on this show, obviously!"

Sparks showed that same punk rock attitude at the 1992 Reading Festival. When people started throwing mud at the band (who couldn't start their set due to sound problems), Sparks got mad, pulled out her tampon and threw it into the crowd. "I did not know I was making rock history at the time, it was just one of those things," Sparks said in the same *Dazed* interview. Yeah, the Sex Pistols would know a thing or two about that...

THE CHRONIC BY DR. DRE

Gangsta rap had been around well before the release of Dr. Dre's solo debut *The Chronic* (1992). Indeed, Dre's work with NWA had gone a long way towards making the genre popular. While the group's first album *Straight Outta Compton* (1988) played a crucial role in defining the sound of West Coast hip-hop, their follow-up *Niggaz4Life* made it to number one on the *Billboard* 200 chart.

These were certainly no small feats, but *The Chronic* might have topped them. The album's laid-back beats, soulful backup vocals, and high-pitched synthesizer chords—all of which drew heavily on the music of George Clinton and Parliament-Funkadelic—would dominate the sound of hip-hop in the years that followed. As music writer Stephen Thomas Erlewine observes, "For the next four years, it was virtually impossible to hear mainstream hip-hop that wasn't affected in some way by Dre and his patented G-funk."

The Chronic wasn't just a major success for Dr. Dre. The album also launched the careers of Snoop Doggy Dogg, Nate Dogg, and Warren G.

Dr. Dre is so closely associated with hardcore hip-hop that his decidedly non-gangsta beginnings may shock some people. In 1984, Dre joined the electro group World Class Wreckin' Cru, whose music was much closer to Chic or Rick James than to NWA. Pictures of him during the time show him wearing shiny red suits (*Complex* picked them as number 41 on their list "The Worst Hip-Hop Fashion Fails of All Time").

EXILE IN GUYVILLE BY LIZ PHAIR

Plenty of people love *Exile on Main St.* (1972). However, few fans can match Liz Phair's obsessive devotion to the Rolling Stones' double-LP masterpiece. How much does Phair love the album, you ask? Well, she called her breakthrough album *Exile in Guyville* (1993) a "track-by-track response" to the record.

"It was conscious the entire time," Phair told *Rolling Stone* in 2010. "A lot of the songs I had already, and I'd put them into slots and move them around. I remember when I got 'Fuck and Run' for 'Happy,' I was like, OK, this totally, totally works. But stuff would shift, then I had to write a few."

Guyville wasn't just an act of adoration, though. It was a declaration of independence too.

"I was so angry about being taken advantage of sexually, being overlooked intellectually," Phair said in the same *Rolling Stone* interview. "A lot of *Exile in Guyville* was about an 'I'll show them.' That was a major emotion in my life, pent up for a long time."

That emotion came through. After more than 20 years, *Guyville* is still Phair's most acclaimed album. Mick Jagger apparently wasn't too impressed, though. Phair remembered meeting him once at the A&M studios in Los Angeles. He struck her as polite but also mildly dismissive. "I wasn't mad," Phair said. "He's Mick!"

AMERICAN RECORDINGS BY JOHNNY CASH

One of the biggest surprises in 90s music was the renewed popularity of Johnny Cash. The country music icon had come up with such pioneering rock and rollers like Elvis Presley and Jerry Lee Lewis, but by the 90s, he was considered a has-been. Columbia Records—Cash's recording home for 26 years— dropped him from their artist roster in 1986. He spent a few years signed to Mercury without much success.

Then Cash met producer Rick Rubin, who was best known for working with groups like the Beastie Boys, the Red Hot Chili Peppers, and Slayer. Not only did Rubin offer him a contract with his label, he had an idea for an album that was music to Cash's ears: No string sections, no backup singers, just the Man in Black and his guitar. Together, the two men made *American Recordings* (1994), which earned rave reviews and introduced Cash to a whole new generation of rockers.

One of the main strengths of *American Recordings* is its eclectic list of songs. Cash sings both his own work and songs by artists like Leonard Cohen, Nick Lowe, and Tom Waits. One of the most unexpected covers was the song "Thirteen" by heavy metal musician Glenn Danzig. According to Danzig, it took him only 20 minutes to write the song!

GRACE BY JEFF BUCKLEY

If you look at pictures of Tim Buckley and his son Jeff, you can definitely see the resemblance. If you listen to each musician's music, not so much.

Rather than emulate his dad's swooning folk, Jeff Buckley's album *Grace* (1993) blends Led Zeppelin-esque rock with touches of soul, blues, and jazz. Its mix of delicacy and thunderous power continues to haunt listeners today. Several artists have written tributes to Buckley, including PJ Harvey, Rufus Wainwright, Courtney Love, Aimee Mann, and Lana Del Rey.

Ironically, a cover of one of Tim Buckley's songs kick-started Jeff's music career. At a tribute to his father, Jeff Buckley sang "I Never Asked to Be Your Mountain," which Tim had written about Jeff and his mom. Well, if he couldn't be his mountain, at least he was his springboard...

LIVE THROUGH THIS BY HOLE

Courtney Love may be her own worst enemy, but boy, has she had some cards dealt against her. Hole's second and best album, *Live Through This* (1994), had the colossally bad luck of coming out one week after her husband Kurt Cobain's suicide. Almost immediately, rumors started spreading that the Nirvana frontman had written the album's songs, not his wife and her bandmates. Thankfully, critics and listeners didn't pay attention to that BS— the album sold well and was voted the best album of the year by *Rolling Stone* and *Village Voice*.

While he didn't write the songs, Cobain did contribute to *Live Through This*—he sang backup vocals on "Asking for It" and "Softer, Softest."

MELLON COLLIE AND THE INFINITE SADNESS BY SMASHING PUMPKINS

Siamese Dream (1993) gave Smashing Pumpkins their mainstream breakthrough, but it wasn't enough for bandleader Billy Corgan. For their follow-up, he had a vision of a sprawling yet unified double album—in his words, "[Pink Floyd's] *The*

Wall for Generation X."

Hubristic? Sure. But here's the thing—he and his bandmates pulled it off! Weighing in at 28 tracks and running the gamut from snarling metal and anthemic hard rock to wistful ballads and bouncy electro-pop, *Mellon Collie and the Infinite Sadness* (1995) racked up seven Grammy nominations and sold more than 10 million albums in the US alone in 1996.

Corgan suffered for his art—he played his guitar so hard on the solo for "Fuck You (An Ode to No One)" that his fingers bled. He didn't shoulder the burden alone, though; unlike *Siamese Dream*—where Corgan played all the guitar and bass parts himself—guitarist James Iha and bassist D'arcy Wretzky played their own parts and helped with arrangements.

ODELAY BY BECK

Mellow Gold (1994) may have been a huge hit for Beck, but it also prompted some people to call him a fake and a one-hit wonder. His sophomore album *Odelay* (1996) shut up the naysayers by mashing together rap, rock, electronica, country, and experimental noise. It topped the *Village Voice* Pazz and Jop poll, was named Album of the Year by *Rolling Stone*, and won a Grammy for Best Alternative Music Album.

Odelay's title comes from the Mexican slang word "órale," which basically means, "What's up?" Pavement frontman Stephen Malkmus told *Spin* in 2011 that it's also a pun on "oh delay." Beck called it that "because it was taking so long to come out."

DIG ME OUT BY SLEATER-KINNEY

Sleater-Kinney received tremendous acclaim for their second album *Call the Doctor* (1996), but their follow-up *Dig Me Out* (1997) had one major advantage: It featured powerhouse drummer Janet Weiss. Band co-founders Corin Tucker and Carrie Brownstein had gone through three previous drummers before meeting Weiss. At her audition for the band, the three musicians tried playing what would become the next album's title track.

"Immediately Janet grounded the song in a way we'd never heard, giving each of our guitar parts a place to go," Brownstein recalls in her 2015 memoir *Hunger Makes Me a Modern Girl*. Weiss' muscular work behind the drum kit would power the rest of *Dig Me Out*, which received even better reviews than its predecessor. It frequently shows up on lists of the best albums of the 90s or of all time.

Dig Me Out's cover indicates that Weiss was (and is) the perfect drummer for Sleater-Kinney. Its three small pictures of the band members over a larger photo of Brownstein's guitar is a tribute to the Kinks' album *The Kink Kontroversy*. Weiss has cited the Kinks, the Rolling Stones, and the Beatles as major influences on her drumming. Some things are just meant to be!

RANDOM FUN FACTS

1. Paul Simon's album *Graceland* had a surprising fan: Clash frontman (and lover of African music) Joe Strummer. "He's hit a new plateau there, but he's writing to his own age group," Stummer told the *Los Angeles Times* in 1988. "*Graceland* is something new. That song to his son is just as good as 'Blue Suede Shoes.'"

2. The Replacements' original name was Dogbreath. It didn't take them too long to realize that they needed a better name, so drummer Chris Mars suggested "The Substitutes." Paul Westerberg played on that and came up with, "The Replacements." Mars wrote in an unpublished memoir, "It seemed to sit just right with us, accurately describing our collective 'secondary' social esteem."

3. The squealing, two-note saxophone hook on Public Enemy's "Rebel Without a Pause" comes from "The Grunt," a 1970 instrumental recorded by James Brown's backing band, the JB's. The record has also been sampled by Eric B. and Rakim, 2 Live Crew, Wu-Tang Clan, and the Black Eyed Peas.

4. "Where is My Mind?" from the album *Surfer Rosa* has turned up in numerous films, TV shows, and commercials. According to Pixies lead singer and songwriter Black Francis (aka Frank Black), the inspiration for the song came

from a time when he was scuba diving in the Caribbean and a small fish tried to chase him. "I don't know why—I don't know too much about fish behavior," he told the UK music magazine *Select* in 1997.

5. Guitarist Ricky Wilson has only one musical credit that isn't a B-52s recording. He played guitar on the song "Breakin' In My Heart" from ex-Television frontman Tom Verlaine's self-titled debut album, which came out in 1979.

6. In addition to music, X bassist John Doe is an actor. He has appeared in such films as *Road House*, *Wyatt Earp*, and *Boogie Nights*.

7. *Flashdance* star Jennifer Beals was initially offered Apollonia Kotero's role in *Purple Rain*. She turned it down because she wanted to finish her college degree.

8. Early copies of *London Calling* didn't list "Train in Vain" on the back cover. That's because the Clash added the song to the album as the sleeves were already being made.

9. Guitarist Robert Quine, who shows up prominently on Lou Reed's *The Blue Mask*, was the second cousin once removed of Dan Auerbach from the Black Keys.

10. The title track of Paul Simon's album *Graceland* features background vocals by the Everly Brothers, who are best known for early rock and roll hits like "Wake Up Little Susie," Bye Bye Love," and "When Will I Be Loved."

11. L7 appears in John Waters' dark 1994 comedy *Serial Mom*

as Camel Lips. "We did a live scene in a club called Hammerjack's, and we had pants that had padded pussies so it was very accentuated," Donita Sparks remembered. "[Waters] wanted us to write a song for the film and said, 'All I care about is that the name of it is "Gas Chamber,"' and I was like, 'OK!'"

12. Born Andre Young, Dr. Dre's original stage name was "Dr. J" after his favorite basketball player, Julius Erving of the Philadelphia 76ers.

13. Sonic Youth's album *Daydream Nation* was engineered by Nick Sansano, who had worked mainly with hip-hop artists like Run DMC and Public Enemy. He didn't really know the band's music, but he knew it was supposed to be intense. To show that he could bring the noise, he showed them his work on "Black Steel in the Hour of Chaos" from *It Takes a Nation of Millions to Hold Us Back*. Sonic Youth dug it, so they recorded their album with Sansano at Greene Street Recording.

14. A year before Johnny Cash put out *American Recordings*, he contributed a guest vocal to the U2 song "The Wanderer."

15. In addition to producing the Jeff Buckley album *Grace*, Andy Wallace also mixed Nirvana's *Nevermind*.

TEST YOURSELF – QUESTIONS AND ANSWERS

1. "I Will Dare" from the Replacements' *Let It Be* features a solo from which acclaimed indie-rock guitarist?

A) Thurston Moore

B) Peter Buck

C) Bob Mould

2. Which REM album features guest vocals from B-52s singer Kate Pierson?

A) Out of Time (1991)
B) *Automatic for the People* (1992)
C) *Reveal* (2001)

3. Nirvana's breakthrough album *Nevermind* was produced by Butch Vig. Which other classic grunge-era album did he produce?

A) Superunknown (1994) by Soundgarden
B) *Ten* (1991) by Pearl Jam
C) *Siamese Dream* (1993) by Smashing Pumpkins

4. X lead singer Exene Cervenka was married to which movie star?

A) Viggo Mortensen
B) Ed Harris
C) Robert Downey Jr.

5. Which rock band plays on "The Myth of Fingerprints" from Paul Simon's *Graceland*?

A) The Blasters

B) The E Street Band

C) Los Lobos

ANSWERS

1. B

2. A

3. C

4. A

5. C

DON'T FORGET YOUR FREE BOOKS

143

MORE BOOKS BY BILL O'NEILL

I hope you enjoyed this book and learned something new. Please feel free to check out some of my previous books.

Made in the USA
Middletown, DE
18 November 2021